THE LIGHTER SIDE

Serving Up Life Lessons with a Smile

Brett Younger

© 2012 Nurturing Faith Inc.

Published in the United States by Nurturing Faith Inc., Macon GA,
www.nurturingfaith.net.

Library of Congress Cataloging-in-Publication Data is available.

ISBN 978-1-938514-02-9

All rights reserved. Printed in the United States of America

Contents

Foreword by Carol, Graham and Caleb Younger   v

Introduction   vii

Baptist Bites

All in the Baptist family	3
A speech you won't hear at the Georgia Baptist Convention	5
The flag that doesn't fly over Harold's head	7
Singing harmony	9
Happy 20th, Cooperative Baptist Fellowship	11

Church Fixins

Regular commitments	15
A guide to excruciatingly correct church behavior	17
My parents' church	19
Windshield wiper wisdom	21
Good book clubs	23
"Anybody could have done it"	25
Down in our hearts	27
Preachers' soles	29

Ministry Menu

The most interesting minister in the world	33
The secret life of preachers	36
Meditation, contemplation, and picante sauce	38
Church shopping	40
Should I have named my son Karl Barth?	42
The former pastors' club	44
The world's best temp job	46

Holiday Staples

Dear Advent Expert	51
Christmas quiz	54
In with the old, in with the new	56
Groundhog Day, Holy Day	58
Dear Lent Expert	60
Pomp and circumstances	63
Why Baptists should do Pentecost	65
Giving thanks in a world of greed	67

Family Favorites

Why I love butter pecan	71
What kind of fiend?	73
Caleb's credit card	75
If you get the chance, dance	79
Celibate celebration	81
Caleb Younger on his father's preaching	83
Life is short	86
Why I am a patient driving instructor	88
A preacher looks at 50	90
My mother, Ginger Rogers	92
The birds and bees (and how they fly)	94
Runaway bunnies	96

Ballpark Fare

Someone left the lights on, and I'm just trying to jog past them	101
In the big inning, God created baseball	103
Like no one's watching	105
Hoop dreams (or nightmares)	107
A warm spot for benchwarmers	109
Service with a smile	111
The audacity of hoops	113
Telling the truth	115
The young and the waistless, the old and the beautiful	117

Regional Specials

Your guide to the Holy Land	121
A preacher goes parrothead	123
Breakfast in Peppertown	125
Bread of heaven	127
Getting our ducks in a row	129
Me and the Boss	131
Up in the air	133

Leftovers

Dancing with the devil	137
Temptation's surprising appearance	139
Life's laundry list	141
Scrubbing the tub	143
The joy of sox	145
Shoe business	147
Shaved by grace	149
Hair today, gone tomorrow	151

Foreword

By Carol, Graham, and Caleb Younger

Some families have a person who never leaves home without a camera. Thick photo albums rest on their coffee tables. Our family has a beloved member who never leaves the house without a pen, a notebook or a handful of index cards — just in case. Our family scrapbooks sit on the bookshelf inside our *Baptists Today* collection.

Sometimes readers of *Baptists Today* ask if our lives are really as glamorous as they are portrayed in "The Lighter Side." We always respond: "Yes." We have walked the red carpet in extravaganzas such as the International Biscuit Festival. We have dined on the fine cuisine the Peppertown Restaurant has to offer. We have visited hotels where regal ducks majestically walk to a large fountain.

Sometimes it can be hard to distinguish where the luxurious column lifestyle and the luxurious lifestyle we hold in reality begin and end. Would Caleb and Graham have sounded so much like Jesus if their dad weren't writing a column? Yes, but not nearly as many people would have heard them.

The truth is that our father/husband doesn't need to fabricate stories because he has a way of making the mundane sparkle. Things become events when he covers them, writing what was there: people overly excited about biscuits; waitresses who believed their job description included getting to know their customers; travelers at the nicest hotel in Memphis, watching ducks with a sense of wonder that seemed out of place.

After 12 years of these candid slices of life, the boy whose tie and button-down shirt made him squirm at a wedding now wears those regularly and will soon be a groomsman for a fellow law student. The 6-year-old who received a credit card offer now receives such mail legitimately, since he is about to enter college. The seminary student who was scooping butter pecan at the Welcome New Students Ice Cream Social in 1983 has resigned herself to knowing that if she books an anniversary getaway at a monastery and ends up in a separate room from her husband, it will show up in a column.

Like all scrapbooks, this one has been fun for us to reread and consider. "Did you really say that?" "Did I really make us do that?" "Did we really think that?" (On a few occasions we suspect the answer is "No.") If life is a scrapbook of moments, this scrapbook makes us grateful for the time we've had and for the one we love who always keeps an extra pen handy to make sure he pays attention to the humor and meaning all around us. These columns make us laugh, but they also help us see the significance of even the lightest moments.

Introduction

I thought about titles for this book that aren't quite right ... *The Lighter Side — Greatest Hits 2000-2012* or *The Lighter Side — Volume 1* or *Lighten Up* or *Columns I Wish Were Funnier* — or one that might help it sell: *Pulitzer Prize-Winning Columns*. Then I found out that I don't get to pick the title.

I'm sure that when Johnny Pierce invited me to write "The Lighter Side" he meant "lighter" as in "not serious." "Not serious" is a fine goal, but writing this column has done surprising things for me.

Because I write this column for *Baptists Today*, I learned that Johnny Cash, the Sundance Kid, and Queen Latifah (think of her as G.A. Queen Latifah-with-a-Scepter) were Baptists. When I heard that the Georgia Baptist Convention was kicking out a church for having a female pastor, I didn't think — as I would have before having this column — "Why are Baptists stupid?" but jumped straight to "Why don't we kick out all women who wear 'braided hair, or gold, or pearls'?" (1 Timothy 2:9).

My light, bright family has been the victim of many columns. I've written about the day I met Carol (she was scooping butter pecan for new seminary students; I got in line even though I prefer chocolate).

I would not have been a chaperone at Graham's sixth grade dance if I wasn't sure I could get a column out of it. (I was kind to shout loud enough for his friends to hear, "I wish your father was here.") When Caleb needed a driving instructor, I agreed because I could write about it: "For future reference, the brake is the one on the left."

When Carol and I spent our 25th wedding anniversary in separate rooms at a monastery, my disappointment was tempered by Carol's assurance that people would laugh at my frustration.

My pathetic attempts at athletics seem less agonizing when I write about them: "The key to my success is not running fast or far." This column inspired me to admit that "Gyms contain little oxygen, and the line between warming up and tiring out is now non-existent."

When I played basketball at youth camp, my pain was tempered by the understanding that I could write about it: "I conserved energy by taking the elevator instead of the stairs and lying down in the shower."

Because I write this column, I took notes during a trip to Israel: "Have you seen any of these in your town — The Church of the Adolescent Jesus, The Church of the Flagellation or The Church of Our Lady of the Spasm?"

I took notes at a Jimmy Buffett concert: "Jimmy claimed the pope came to a concert, blessed the cheeseburgers and told Jimmy he had long been a parrothead."

I took notes at the International Biscuit Festival (which I would never have attended if I did not write this column): "BYOB — Butter Your Own Biscuit."

I have learned to look for the shining lights in Christ's church — gracious women who wish Miss Manners had written Romans, the painter at my parents' church who put a hint of kudzu in the baptistery, the good church people who made me drive home barefoot after preaching at their church because they thought someone in Liberia needed my shoes more than I do.

I have learned to look for the bright lights in ministry: the kind of preachers whose nurseries run out of space nine months after they preach on the Song of Solomon; ministers who speak on war, abortion, and the presidential campaign and have everyone shouting "Amen"; ministers who may initially be distracted during worship ("Why does the Lord's Prayer sound like the voice on my GPS?"), but who end up with "I can't believe what saints I get to serve."

When I joined the Former Pastors' Club, this column led me to make a list of what I missed — baptizing young Christians, senior citizens who ask me to pray with them and free parking at the hospital.

When you write a column called "The Lighter Side," you end up looking for light. I have been given a good gift.

Baptist Bites

All in the Baptist family
January 2006

It isn't easy being Baptist. I've asked non-Baptist ministers to preach at our church about 10 times. The conversation goes something like this:

"You want a Methodist/Disciple/Presbyterian/fill-in-the-blank to preach at a Baptist church?"

"Yes, that's why I asked you."

"I've never preached at a Baptist church. Can I borrow your overalls?"

While many Baptist churches are filled with intelligent, sophisticated people, Baptists as a group don't have the most cultured reputation. I'd like to complain, but it's hard for even lifelong Baptists to know how to categorize us. Baptists are a mixed bag.

Politically speaking, we're all over the map. Jesse Helms is a Baptist, but so is Jesse Jackson. Tom DeLay is a Baptist, as is Al Gore. If that's not confusing enough, two of four Baptist presidents (Warren Harding and Bill Clinton) had scandals that embarrassed the WMU, but the other two (Jimmy Carter and Harry Truman) would make fine presidents of the Brotherhood.

Contrary to some opinions, Baptists not only read but also write. John Bunyan (*Pilgrim's Progress*), Oswald Chambers (*My Utmost for His Highest*), Will Campbell (*Brother to a Dragonfly*) and John Grisham (*A Time to Kill*— not a particularly Baptist book, but it sold pretty well) are Baptists.

Preacher wise, you can pick and choose who you're proud to say is a Baptist: Martin Luther King Jr., Billy Graham, Walter Rauschenbusch, Harry Emerson Fosdick, Rick Warren, Charles Haddon Spurgeon and Jerry Falwell. (Picture those seven sharing a table at the prayer breakfast.)

Johnny Cash was a Baptist — enough to put to rest the idea that Baptists are dull. If there's a Baptist choir in heaven, it will be amazing: Aretha Franklin, Diana Ross, Whitney Houston, Donna Summer, Mahalia Jackson, Bill Haley, Buddy Holly, Otis Redding, Al Green, Chuck Berry, George Jones, Roy Orbison and Hank Williams Sr. (I'm guessing Hank Jr. doesn't make it to church most Sundays, but I could be wrong.) Louis Armstrong can play the trumpet, Glen Campbell the guitar, and Van Cliburn the piano.

Baptists may be better musicians than athletes, but Joe Frazier, Jim Brown, Reggie White, Payne Stewart and Maury Wills were Baptists.

Queen Latifah is a Baptist (try picturing her as G.A. Queen Latifah-with-a-Scepter). Baptist parents can decide if they want to tell their children that Jessica Simpson is a Baptist. Harry Longbaugh, the Sundance Kid, was a Baptist. (I realize he was a bank robber, but isn't it encouraging that Robert Redford played a Baptist?)

Ava Gardner was a Baptist, but Howard Hughes wasn't. Sometimes I wish more Baptists were rich like Baptist John D. Rockefeller.

Chuck Norris could have starred in *Walker, Texas Baptist*. You can argue that DeForest Kelley, Dr. "Bones" McCoy on *Star Trek*, is the best-known Baptist of the 25th century. I like to think that the Baptist in Kevin Costner is responsible for *Field of Dreams*, and that during *Waterworld* he wasn't going to church much. Kevin was directed by a Baptist, Ron Shelton, in *Bull Durham*, a movie my Baptist mother would not want me to see.

Imagine throwing a "Baptists Only" party and having this crowd show up: Pat Robertson, Bill Moyers, Sam Rayburn, Trent Lott, Anita Bryant, Clarence Thomas, Marian Wright Edelman, Marian Anderson, Gene Autry, Kris Kristofferson and Eddie Murphy.

Some historians claim that Czar Alexander I of Russia was secretly a Baptist. If he was and didn't want people to know, it's understandable. Our family is hard to explain.

A speech you won't hear at the Georgia Baptist Convention
June 2010

The Georgia Baptist Convention is at it again. In November they plan to disfellowship (is that even a word?) Druid Hills Baptist Church in Atlanta for the crime of calling a female co-pastor. It does not matter that Rev. Mimi Walker is a committed minister who preaches the Gospel with passion and integrity. After being excommunicated, the GBC will refuse to accept funds from the 96-year-old congregation, but, interestingly, they will not return the money the church has given to the GBC since Mimi began serving in 2008. I have been thinking about the expulsion of my good friend and her good church and have been trying to imagine how the argument could become any more foolish. Here's a speech that will not be given at the Georgia Baptist Convention, but you are welcome to borrow it if you want to try:

"Mr. President, distinguished messengers and other Bible-believing Georgians, I rejoice that Georgia Baptists are spreading the gospel from Rome to Valdosta, Columbus to Savannah, Atlanta to Augusta, Athens to Americus, in Ellijay, Enigma, Fargo, Cairo, Egypt, Damascus, Sparta, Glory, Hephzibah, Hiawassee and Daisy. The gospel is being shared with old and young, rich and poor, conservative and more conservative, native Georgian and foreign interloper.

"I stand to commend this august body for taking seriously the admonition in 1 Timothy 2:11-12, and I read, as all Christians should, from the King James Version, 'Let the woman learn in silence with all subjection. But I suffer not a woman to teach, nor to usurp authority over the man, but to be in silence.' We follow this infallible commandment joyfully, but this chapter has 15 verses and each one of them is equally inspired and inerrant. This leads to my distress that we're not taking the whole Bible seriously enough.

"Immediately following, in verses 13 and 14, we read, 'For Adam was first formed, then Eve. And Adam was not deceived, but the woman being deceived was in the transgression.' (This is, of course, obvious. Verse 15 is the one heretics overlook.) 'Notwithstanding she shall be saved in childbearing, if they continue in faith and charity and holiness with sobriety.'

"You may be saying, 'What about Lottie Moon? Lottie didn't have children.' (Mother Teresa didn't have children either, but she was a Catholic — enough said.) I know there are liberals who would like for God to make an exception for Lottie (also Dolly Parton), but the Bible says it. I believe it. That settles it.

"My greater concern is the passage a few sentences earlier — 1 Timothy 2:9 — 'women should adorn themselves in modest apparel, with shamefacedness and sobriety; not with braided hair, or gold, or pearls, or costly array.'

"We're all for 'modest apparel, with shamefacedness and sobriety' and I am no fan of 'braided hair,' but the 'gold or pearls' part may be problematic at some otherwise acceptable Georgia Baptist churches.

"It may be hard for you to imagine upstanding Christian women not wearing wedding rings, but that's what it says. First Timothy also clearly prohibits True Love Waits purity rings. We need to warn and punish those who sinfully wear gold cross earrings.

"One group that has been given far too long to repent is Girls in Action. When a G.A. reaches the level of Queen Regent-with-a-Scepter, why can't she be honored without the wicked use of gold? What are we teaching tomorrow's WMU?

"I've heard about a church where the pastor gives those who are baptized a gold necklace with the Christian fish symbol. Those corrupt churches will be more comfortable in the Episcopal Church.

"You may have some anxiety for the people who work in James Avery's 'Christian jewelry' division, but they are an abomination. Perhaps they could switch to printing 1 Timothy 2:9 on plastic bracelets.

"I know that some will think it harsh when we kick out all of the churches where women wear gold, but if we're going to be honest and consistent, we have no choice."

The flag that doesn't fly over Harold's bed
November 2010

On the Sunday before Veterans Day, Harold was thinking about the flag while his pastor was preaching about following Christ or commitment to God alone or something like that. Why couldn't they put some bunting on the pulpit? Wouldn't it be great to sing "I'm Proud to Be an American" instead of the "Doxology"? What would be the harm in saying the Pledge of Allegiance together?

Harold thinks of himself as a war hero. He spent the last three months of the Korean War at Fort Benning, Ga., cooking breakfast — powdered eggs, grits, toast, sausage and, on Saturdays, pancakes. He lives in fear that people will forget the sacrifices he made.

Harold didn't usually get in line to shake the preacher's hand, but he decided to hang around today. He listened as people offered the usual comments: "I enjoyed the service," "You really stepped on their toes today," "Nice weather we're having," "Better luck next time."

Most people tried to say something related to the sermon, but Harold had something important to get off his chest: "Pastor, we need a flag in our sanctuary. We need it now. I'm ready to pay for it. We need a flag to tell everyone who comes to our church that we're Americans and darn proud of it."

The pastor's mind races to possible responses. He could try to explain again that Baptists were founded on the ideal of the separation of church and state. For 400 years Baptists have refused to allow loyalty to any country to be on equal footing with loyalty to Christ. Harold had been around for a pretty significant portion of Baptist history. He should know this by now.

The pastor could talk about the symbols at the front of their sanctuary — a communion table, a baptistery, a Bible and a cross. Did any country's flag — even their favorite country's — belong with the emblems of a faith that knows no borders? Harold loves NASCAR. Would he want a picture of Dale Earnhardt in the baptistery? Christians love Jesus' mother. How would Harold feel about a statue of Mary on the communion table?

The pastor could mention Reina, the Japanese exchange student living with the Petersons for a year. Reina's parents are Buddhist. What message will she get if there's an American flag in the only Christian place of worship she's ever visited? If Baptists believe in the priesthood of every believer, doesn't that include the believer who isn't American? What does it mean if a flag in a church represents only a portion of believers? Harold is a proud graduate of the University of Georgia. Would he also like a UGA pennant in the sanctuary? What if the chair of deacons pushed for an NC State banner?

The pastor could have raised any of these serious questions, but then the oddest thought popped into the pastor's head and out of his mouth before he could stop it: "Harold, do you and Lucille have an American flag over your bed?"

"What?"

"Is there an American flag pinned to the ceiling over your bed?"

Harold was confused, "No."

"Is it because you don't love our country?"

"No, that's ridiculous."

"So you're telling me that the absence of a flag over your bed isn't an indication of your lack of patriotism."

"No, of course not."

"Why do your refuse to put a flag over your bed?"

Harold's face was red, white and blue, "I don't refuse to put a flag over my bed. It just doesn't belong there."

"Harold, I'm disappointed that you're not more patriotic. A flag in your bedroom will tell everyone that you're an American and darn proud of it."

"Wait a second, pastor. You're missing the point."

"When you are in bed, the flag will remind you and Lucille that you're not only committed to each other, but also to the United States of America. I'm ready to pay for it."

"Just forget it. We'll talk again on Memorial Day."

Singing harmony
March 2008

I confess that I usually sing the melody, but not too many Sundays ago I sat by Jeff Newton. During the second stanza of "My Jesus, I Love Thee" I realized that while I was making a dull unison contribution, Jeff was taking off on the tenor line. By the time we got to "If ever I loved thee, my Jesus, 'tis now," I was doing my best to add the bass line. Unison is easier, but at the best churches — in our best moments — we sing harmony.

Churches should be more spirited harmonization than unthinking agreement, more Baskin Robbins than plain vanilla. Not "My way or the highway," but "Our way is spaghetti junction." Diversity is more complicated, but it's also more interesting. It's a small church that only has room for one set of opinions.

When visitors come, we should be able to say: "We've got people like you. We have Huckabees and Hillaries. We drive Lexuses, Priuses and don't drive at all. We watch *Washington Week in Review* and *American Gladiators*. We listen to Mendelssohn and Willie Nelson. We went to *The Great Debaters* and *Alvin and the Chipmunks*. We have Dallas Cowboys fans and those who have learned to keep their opinions to themselves."

We sing harmony, because we're the church. The best churches encourage creativity and new ideas. It takes courage to bless a variety of opinions, but Carlyle Marney said, "The church that has not lost its courage will never have to advertise its location."

We sing harmony, because we're Baptist. One of the best things about having no creed but the Bible is that you end up meeting such interesting people at church. The people with whom we disagree are often the ones from whom we can learn the most. In real Baptist churches, members are forever saying, "I won't let our differences get in the way of our friendship."

We sing harmony, because we're following Jesus. If you take seriously the hard questions of discipleship, you have to make room for answers that aren't always simple. The Kingdom of God is bigger than we have imagined. When we discover a difference of opinion, it's an opportunity to go beyond merely tolerating one another to celebrating our diversity.

When people suggest that churches have to be all this or all that, those who sing harmony know it isn't true. A choir with only tenors isn't really a choir. Christ's followers listen carefully to one another and add our different parts to the one song.

Christians have different perspectives on the incarnation, but we all sing "Silent Night." Christians have a variety of ideas on the atonement, but we all sing "When I Survey the Wondrous Cross." Christians may disagree on what the resurrection looked like, but we all sing "Christ the Lord Is Risen Today." Christians have different lists of who gets into heaven, but we sing "Amazing Grace" together.

The best churches are big enough for everyone who wants to sing of Christ. What holds us together is the affirmation "Jesus is Lord." God calls us to be loyal to Christ before anything else — even before our opinions. We don't have to sing the same notes at the same time. We just have to sing the song of God's love together.

Illustration by Scott Brooks

Happy 20th, Cooperative Baptist Fellowship
July 2011

In 1991 the final episode of *Dallas* aired, the Chicago Bulls won their first championship, Arnold Schwarzenegger starred in *Terminator 2* and the Cooperative Baptist Fellowship began. All of this is ancient history to most of my students. Just as someone needs to explain J.R., M.J. and why bodybuilders should not be governors, we need to keep telling the Baptist story.

Baptists find their beginnings in the Anabaptists of 16th-century Europe. They fought for religious freedom and an absolute separation of church and state that would have driven Jerry Falwell crazy. The British Baptists of the 17th century refused to fill out membership cards for the state-controlled Church of England. Thomas Helwys was criticized for defending religious liberty for atheists, Jews and Muslims. (Imagine the reaction if Joel Osteen defended Charlie Sheen.) King James, who clearly had not read the more gracious portions of the King James Bible, sent Helwys to jail where the Baptist preacher died.

Roger Williams is often called the father of the Baptist movement in America, even though shortly after starting the First Baptist Church in America in 1638 he gave up on Baptists for not being radical enough. He argued for making recompense to Native Americans for taking their land. That was hard for the Baptists on the finance committee to take.

Up until the 1800s, Baptists in the United States would not join together in a national body, because they were afraid of becoming too organized. Some argue that Baptists might have been better off if they had never gotten over this fear of large organizations.

When the Civil War began, Baptists in the South took a firm stand for what they believed. Unfortunately, they believed in slavery.

When the war was over, Baptists began overwhelming the South in a way that would have made Sherman envious. By the 1970s there were more Baptists in the South than there were people. Baptists ruled the land, but they wanted to rule one another. New pseudo-Baptists decided that all Baptists had to think the same.

In 1979 an uncivil war broke out. The fundamentalists said it was about the inerrancy of the Bible. The old-time Baptists said it was about the priesthood of the believer. We fought over *The Baptist Faith & Message*, which was not supposed to be a creed, as though it was a creed. We surprisingly decided that Jesus is not "the criterion by which Scripture is to be interpreted." We argued over whether God was allowed to call a woman to be a minister and if we were allowed to go to Disneyworld.

For 10 years the moderates struggled to hold things together, but it was not to be. The potentates who took over the Southern Baptist Convention were not paying attention in their Baptist heritage class. The new SBC would not be Southern in the hospitable sense of the word or Baptist in the historic sense of the word or what you would hope for in a convention.

The painful process of deciding who gets which kids began. They got Adrian Rogers. We got Melissa Rogers. They got Jimmy Draper. We got Jimmy Allen. They got Jim Henry. We got Jim Dunn. They got Bailey Smith. We got to keep our Jewish friends. They got the buildings at Glorieta and Ridgecrest. We didn't. They got the seminaries. We got the professors. They got new seminary presidents like Al Mohler. We got new seminary presidents like Molly Marshall. They got 44,000 churches. We got about 1,900 — admittedly less.

Since 1991, Cooperative Baptists have been creating a new yet old way to be Baptist. CBF works with a commitment to global missions, missional churches, women in ministry, theological education and intellectual freedom. Being marginalized leads to creativity. Churches are doing new, exciting, incarnational, Kingdom ministries. Connections are being made between churches and missions. God is at work.

CBF is not as big as some might hope and not as radical as Roger Williams might wish, but if the fundamentalists had not taken over the Southern Baptist Convention, I wonder if I would still be a Baptist. While it is easy for Baptists to remember the good old days fondly, the SBC of 1978 was not particularly diverse, affirming of women or open to new ideas. I will keep trying to explain to my students that history matters. The CBF is not only a new family, but also the reason some of us have a family. We need to tell that story.

Church Fixins

Regular commitments
August 2005

It's always seemed out of reach, but one of my dreams has been to be some restaurant's "regular." I have lots of excuses for never becoming a regular. It's hard to be a regular when you don't eat out very often. It's difficult to find the right place. Lots of restaurants don't have regulars. Nonetheless, I never completely gave up my dream of a place where the waitress knows my name.

Some time ago Carol and I started acting a little like regulars. We were, I see in retrospect, flirting with the commitment. We'd been going to a pancake house about once a month. We always sat in the same booth — second from the end on the right. We always had the same excellent waitress. We once saw her line up five plates on her arm. She claims a record of 12, but we have yet to see it. We weren't completely committed, but in the deep recesses of our hearts, I believe we were preparing to be regulars.

Then our church secretary generously gave us gift certificates to that same pancake house. What more obvious sign could there have been that it was time to step across the line from guest to regular? There was almost immediate progress. The manager greeted us with "Hey guys!" Our waitress figured out that I want my coffee refilled only once.

Of course, we've had setbacks, like the painful morning when the man behind the counter said: "We have booths and tables. Take your pick." I wanted to shout, "We know you have booths and tables! We're almost regulars!"

At times, becoming a regular has been frightening. On one occasion our waitress didn't bring us menus. We didn't want to ask for them (regulars shouldn't need menus), but we weren't ready for such a big step.

We've learned about the disadvantages of being a regular. Regulars have to leave bigger tips. It takes longer for regulars to order, because we need to ask, "How are you doing?" and listen to the response. While few expectations are put on a guest, a regular is expected to be friendly even when not feeling friendly. Getting to know people is always a mixed blessing. We are glad to know that our waitress has children, but sad to hear when one is sick.

Overall, this has been a good experience for us. I can't tell you how impressed my brother-in-law was when our waitress brought us a decaf and a "leaded" before we sat down.

Then came that holy moment when Carol and I became genuine regulars. For the first time, our waitress brought the wrong order (pancakes instead of eggs). We decided that she was having a bad day. We would eat what she brought and leave an extra large tip. This doesn't sound like a particularly inspiring story, but it has led us to the conclusion that being a regular is worth the cost.

On Sundays, most churches are a mix of regulars and guests. There are undeniable advantages to being a guest. Guests aren't expected to know names, give money or serve on a committee. It takes a commitment to be a regular, and getting to know people is always a mixed blessing. It seems likely that the great majority of the people who read *Baptists Today* are some church's "regulars." Every once in a while we need to remember that being a regular is worth the cost. In some ways, it's a dream come true.

A guide to excruciatingly correct church behavior
September 2011

You don't need me to tell you about Judith Martin's *Miss Manners' Guide to Excruciatingly Correct Behavior*. You may have read it more than once. Perhaps you have underlined portions for your children or spouse. We love Miss Manners' strong opinions.

For instance, if you have not yet sent a thank-you letter for any gift you received more than 30 minutes ago, Miss Manners has no mercy on you. You are also in trouble if you sent your thank you via e-mail, Facebook or Twitter. There is, in Miss Manners' world, no such thing as a thank-you *note*. You must begin your thank-you *letter* with a "burst of enthusiasm" and make sure it "names the present with a flattering adjective." When one of her gentle readers confides that she has only green ink with which to write, Miss Manners tells her that she must save all of her letters until Christmas.

The use of tacky note cards and brightly colored ink are not the only subjects about which Miss Manners expresses strong feelings. The only excuse for declining an invitation to be a pallbearer is "a plan to have one's own funeral in the near future." Don't wear black to a wedding. If you are in deep mourning, you should not come in the first place. Even the young are expected to act with extreme manners. When a 6-year-old reader asks what is important enough to tell his mother when she is talking to company, Miss Manners provides a short list that includes "Mommy, the kitchen is full of smoke."

Good rules come in handy. They help things go smoothly. What would Judith Martin include if she decided to help church people with *Miss Manners' Guide to Excruciatingly Correct Church Behavior*?

If you are in your 80s, come to Sunday school early. If you are in your 50s, be on time. If you are in your 20s, everyone will be overjoyed if you show up at all.

You may take coffee to Sunday school. If you bring Starbucks, pour it into a different cup so you will not look uppity. Bring the donuts when it is your turn; Krispy Kremes are preferable. Adults never promote to another Sunday school class. It makes the others in the class feel bad.

Women are encouraged to wear hats at Easter. Men are encouraged to wear hats at church softball games. You can wear flip-flops in the sanctuary only if your mother is not the kind of person who reads Miss Manners.

Be on time for worship. This means *before* the music begins. The first note on the organ, piano or guitar is not a starter's pistol for the hundred-yard dash.

Children need to learn the sacred nature of worship. This means no chewing gum, iPods or iPhones. Stare with disdain at anyone whose cell phone rings.

Try not to draw attention to yourself by singing louder than any three people on your pew. The only satisfactory excuses for not singing are life-threatening conditions. If you only have green ink, it is perfectly acceptable for filling out a check.

When faced with the question of what is important enough to whisper to the gentle worshipper seated next to you, it must be as crucial as "Mommy, the sanctuary is full of smoke." When speaking to the pastor after worship, begin with a "burst of enthusiasm" and "a flattering adjective" in relation to the sermon. After a particularly offensive sermon, use a side exit.

As far as I know, Miss Manners has not written any rules for proper church behavior so it might be helpful to look to someone like Saint Paul for guidance. In Romans 12, he writes: "Let love be genuine. Outdo one another in showing concern. Put others above yourself. Extend hospitality to strangers. Pay no special attention to the wealthy. Talk just as much to the poor. Go out of your way to be kind."

When Paul writes rules for correct church behavior, he sounds like my mother: "Be kind. Be sweet. Love everybody. Don't say mean things. Make sure visitors feel welcome." Maybe we don't need Miss Manners after all.

My parents' church
February 2005

Attending Providence Baptist Church in Tremont, Miss., as my family was privileged to do, is no longer like a trip to the 1950s. They now have carpeting, paneling and microphones — none of which they need. Thankfully some things, like the Sunday school board, haven't changed. The wooden scoreboard proudly proclaims:

SUNDAY SCHOOL
Attendance Today 23
Offering Today $225.00
Attendance Last Sunday 22
Offering Last Sunday $224.00
Preaching Attendance Today 42
Preaching Attendance Offering
(This must not have been impressive as it went unrecorded.)

A plaque near the door lists the Building Committee (1956) — most of whom we met. The church covenant reminds everyone of their promise to "abstain from the sale and use of intoxicating drinks as a beverage." Sign-up sheets offer opportunities to clean up (Ida does most of the cleaning), trim (Charles is the only one who has signed up) and leaf blow. The painting in the baptistery depicts pine trees along the banks of the Jordan River (and I think I may have seen a hint of kudzu).

There was no printed order of worship, because everyone had it memorized. During the prelude we were reminded that the nursery is on the back pew. After the prelude someone asked, "What was that, Helen?" We sang the first, second and fourth stanzas of "I Am Thine, O Lord" from shape note hymnals without anyone telling us to sing the first, second and fourth stanzas. The announcements didn't last long, but the prayer concerns did. Then we sang first, second and fourth of "Are You Washed in the Blood?"

Brother Leon asked Brother Henry and Brother Jerry to take up the offering. When the preacher announced the scripture reading, everybody started turning pages in their King James Bibles. The sermon was on Philip's words to Nathanael, "Come and see." We were encouraged to invite others to "come and see" during that week's revival services.

We sang the first two stanzas of "Have Thine Own Way, Lord." I embarrassed myself by beginning the fourth stanza. I forgot that the invitation always ends after the second stanza on which no one comes forward. The benediction began with "Does anybody want to say a word?" and ended with "See you tonight at 6:00."

Worship at Providence is mostly sweet and sentimental to me, but there are sacred moments. I loved the song Helen sang for the special music: "There'll be no tears to fill our eyes in the place beyond the Jordan River. That sounds like home to me, like where I want to be."

The heart of our rituals and the hope of our worship is the God to whom we can always go home.

Windshield wiper wisdom
November 2009

The rain started before we left home and continued almost all the way. After four hours I optimistically switched to "intermittent," but we spent most of the day on the fast end of the wiper speed dial. I announced several times — to no one's amusement — "The last time it rained like this, Noah built himself a boat."

One hundred miles from our destination, the wiper blade on the passenger's side decided it had had enough and started unraveling. By the time we got to my parents' house, the wiper was almost completely gone.

The next morning we drove through the rain to the Texaco in Mantachie, Mississippi. They only had one blade in stock (it was for a pick-up), but they helpfully pointed us to Jerry Pitts' Auto Parts.

Lines in Mississippi are short, but move slowly. The person in front of us talked to Betty Pitts about the weather ("Wet enough for you?"), somebody's cousin (it was never clear whose) and a lively debate over who fries the best catfish (the consensus is "the place in Centerville, but it's overpriced at $6"). I don't think the person in front of us bought any parts.

When it was our turn, Betty and my father discussed at length how good Amy, Betty's daughter, was in the Tupelo Community Theater presentation of *Annie, Get Your Gun*. When we finally got to the reason for our visit, Betty suggested we replace just the wiper blade rather than the whole assembly, because "that will be cheaper." I took the thin piece of plastic and a borrowed pair of pliers, and promptly broke the thingamajig that holds the wiper (I use non-technical terms so as not to confuse lay readers).

Betty then gave me a metal dilly that she assured us "will snap right on." The rain was coming down hard. I held a borrowed umbrella as my father tried to get the assembly to "snap right on." After awhile he held the umbrella and I tried. Finally we sheepishly asked Betty for help. She knew far more than we did, but — and this made us feel better — she couldn't get it on either.

Betty summoned an innocent bystander who had the misfortune to be in the area. I tried to keep the umbrella over as much of him as I could, but Douglas is big and it was pouring. By the time he announced, "I got it," the stranger who replaced my wiper was soaked.

Betty said, "I'm real sorry that the assembly costs more than just the wiper." She explained with concern that my bill would be $5.44 rather than the original $3.74.

I asked, "How much do I owe for installation?"

Betty smiled as she said, "I don't know where you're from young man, but you're in Mantachie, Mississippi, now."

Isn't that a great line? Wouldn't that be a wonderful line for us to use in our churches?

When a poor person says, "I was surprised that people made me feel so welcome," we can reply, "I don't know where you're from, but you're at church now."

When a hurting person says, "I'm not used to people caring for me," we can respond, "I don't know where you're from, but you're at church now."

When anyone says, "The people here seem to be having such fun," we can smile when we say, "I don't know where you're from, but you're at church now."

Wouldn't it be wonderful?

Good book clubs
December 2007

The cashier asked, with what I am fairly certain was sarcasm, "What movie did you say?"

I couldn't quite look him in the eye, "I said *The Jane Austen Book Club*."

He handed me a pink ticket as though I had more sensibility than sense, offered a tissue and suggested I try the quiche at the concession stand.

He had a point. I left my pride and prejudice in the lobby as Carol and I walked into a testosteroneless theater. Imagine the crowd at *Saw IV*. This was the opposite. The one other male in the room looked uncomfortable until the movie started. That's when he left and went to *American Gangster*.

The Jane Austen Book Club — which one critic called "the movie equivalent of a toenail painting session" — is about Starbucks, knitting, sunny porches, the sensitivity of females and the insensitivity of males. The smart characters, all of whom are female, drink from champagne flutes and use words like "elegiac."

One woman, Prudie, has the misfortune to be married to a guy who confuses Austen with the capital of Texas and likes basketball. What a Neanderthal!

The plot surrounds a group of six (five Jane freaks and one sci-fi geek) who read the six novels of Jane Austen over six months. The prissy woman who knows the most facts about Jane Austen teaches literature, but experiences little of the feeling that enlivens the novels. It's telling that she likes to speak French, but she hasn't been to France.

The one male in the group has never read the books. His first question is, "Are they sequels?" Later he suggests there are parallels to *Star Wars*. Though he may not know the words, he knows the tune. He lives with the depth of feeling that Austen describes and leads the iciest member of the group to risk opening her heart.

The movie works because you get the feeling that unlike most book clubs in movies, they are really reading the books. What makes it interesting is the way the readers' lives start to mirror the characters in the books. The novels begin reflecting their own experiences. At one point, Sylvia (who has just been dumped by Jimmy Smits) says, "I feel like Fanny

Price from Mansfield Park." They share not only Austen's stories, but also the places where the novels intersect with their own hard-won wisdom. Good books and good book clubs change us.

Why can't Sunday school be a really good book club? Why can't more churchgoers understand that we don't study together to learn facts about the Bible, but to experience the life that the scriptures describe and lead one another to risk opening our hearts?

We know prissy people who know lots of details about the Bible, but show no signs of loving anyone. We also know amazing people who can't name any book in the Bible, but live the grace of God.

In the movie, when one of the characters faces an important decision — whether to cheat on her husband — she stops at a busy intersection across from the hotel and sees a "Walk" / "Don't Walk" sign that flashes "What would Jane do?" She turns around, goes home and reads Austen's *Persuasion* to her husband, because it's about a married couple persuading themselves to give it another try.

Why can't we read the Bible together, because we face important questions? The process of sharing the scriptures could help us learn to live and love more fully. We could open our hearts to the Word of God and one another. We could let God persuade us to give it another try.

"Anybody could have done it"
March 2006

I'm not sure how this happened. This is so not me. When I received my car registration renewal from the Texas Department of Motor Vehicles, I immediately sent it in. I was pleased to receive my sticker well before the expiration date.

That's when the story gets fuzzy. As best I can reconstruct it, I inexplicably scraped off the sticker that looked most like the one I had received in the mail and replaced it, without recognizing that I now had two registration stickers and no inspection sticker.

(If you have done this, it would be nice if you would let me know. I will not tell anyone except my wife, Carol, as she seems to need evidence that I'm not the only one this foolish.)

I realized my mistake, but it took a while. I stared at my windshield in disbelief for a long time. Later that morning I pulled in to the "In-N-Out Lube" and tried to explain, "The goofiest thing happened."

Jerry, my mechanic, gently interrupted: "It certainly did. Anybody could have done it. It really is confusing. We get at least three or four of these a week."

John, the smirking teenager standing behind Jerry, did not seem to agree that anybody could have done it or that it's really confusing. John was more of the opinion that it takes a special brand of ineptitude to scrape off your inspection sticker and replace it with a second registration.

I handed Jerry my receipt from two months earlier (at least I'm an idiot who saves receipts) and he graciously said, "We don't have a choice. We have to do the inspection again, but we can shave a few dollars off of this. The government does the dangdest things. It's just ridiculous how much these look alike. At least now your registration and inspection will be the same month. That's an advantage."

I'm still not clear on how this is an advantage, but I am grateful to Jerry for being kind, and I'm more confident than ever about my radiator, power steering and brake fluids.

"Anybody could have done it" and "It really is confusing" are such Christian things to say. Jerry made me think about other gracious comments we can use when confronted with stupid behavior. Some of these suggestions are pretty specific.

"I think I have a coupon for tattoo removal."
"I can hardly see the stain."
"It's going to grow back."
"You were too cute for him."
"You didn't like working there anyway. You said a monkey could do that job."
"I've read that the SAT is a terrible predictor of college success."
"I wrecked my first car when I was 16, too."
"Most men your age look funny in shorts."

Some kind comments after stupid behavior would be helpful around the church:

"Not every sermon has to be thought-provoking."
"The Bible says, 'Make a joyful noise.' You certainly did that."
"It's not like you're the first person to fall asleep during a prayer."
"Bless your heart." (This one works particularly well when spoken by a Southern woman.)

Sometimes a mistake is an opportunity to speak sacred words:

"I know how you're feeling. I've been there, too."
"You made a mistake, but it's not who you are."
"No matter what, I will always be here for you."
"All I want you to do is come home."

Down in our hearts
March 2003

When I was in the primary department in Sunday school, between beginners and juniors, one of my favorite songs was "I've Got the Joy." I'm not sure who wrote the words, but it sounds like it could have been penned by Elizabeth Barrett Browning:

> *I've got the joy, joy, joy, joy down in my heart.*
> *Where?*
> *Down in my heart.*
> *Where?*
> *Down in my heart.*
> *I've got the joy, joy, joy, joy down in my heart.*
> *Down in my heart to stay.*

The first stanza alone is enough to qualify the song as a classic, but the best part is the last verse:

> *And if the devil doesn't like it, he can sit on a tack.*
> *Ouch!*
> *Sit on a tack.*
> *Ouch!*
> *Sit on a tack.*
> *Ouch!*
> *And if the devil doesn't like it, he can sit on a tack.*
> *Sit on a tack to stay.*

The last verse was wonderful not only for the lucidity of the poetry and the insightfulness of the theology, but also for its participatory nature. We began the song seated. Then when we shouted "Ouch!" we jumped out of our chairs. When it was over, everyone in the primary department rolled on the floor and laughed uproariously at how accurately we had depicted what it would look like if the personification of evil did indeed sit on a tack.

When I was about 11 years old, and in the junior department, soon to be an intermediate, the group Three Dog Night recorded a song titled "Joy to the World." The first line was not, however, "Joy to the world, the Lord is come" but was instead, and those of you who have as little musical taste as I have will remember this:

Jeremiah was a bullfrog,
was a good friend of mine.
I never understood a single word he said,
but I helped him drink his wine.

The last line was equally memorable:

Joy to the fishies in the deep blue sea,
joy to you and me.

I bought the 45 record, put the little plastic disk in to make it fit our stereo and, for the first time, invited my mother into my room to listen to my new record. I said, "Look, Mom, I bought 'Joy to the World.' That's one of your favorite Christmas carols, isn't it?" My mother expressed amazement and suggested, as I hoped she would, that we listen to it. Mom left during, "I never understood a single word he said" long before "Joy to the fishies in the deep blue sea." I, of course, rolled on the floor and laughed uproariously.

It's been 27 years since I graduated from the intermediate department. Now when I sing of joy it's in a different key. I no longer find much joy in taunting either the devil or my mother, though both of those activities have their place. Joy is now less like uproarious laughter and more like sustaining hope.

Some things aren't as simple as they once were. I realize now that not all of my dreams will come true. I've seen some of the people I love hurt terribly. I have a few scars of my own. Some of the people I've loved have died. I think that when we realize that life is hard and won't be everything we've hoped, our joy either fades away or goes deeper.

Most recent hymnals include "Joy to the World" — the Isaac Watts version, not the Three Dog Night version — but omit what used to be the third verse: "No more let sins and sorrows grow, nor thorns infest the ground; He comes to make his blessings flow, far as the curse is found." I'm sure the editors think that most congregations don't really enjoy singing: "Far as the curse is found." But it may be that Isaac Watts understood that real joy is found on the other side of the sorrows that grow and the thorns that destroy. God is the great joy deep inside us — the joy, joy, joy, joy down in our hearts. And if the devil doesn't like it, he can sit on a tack.

Preachers' soles
December 2011

She asked as though it is a common concern, "Do I have to wear shoes when I preach?"

Seminary students pose odd questions before preaching in class: "Can I tell the parable from the fatted calf's viewpoint?" "Can I dance my sermon?" "Can I show a clip from *Glee*?" (The answer to these is "No.") This was the first question on footwear. The issues surrounding preachers' shoes are woefully neglected. Ministers who ignore the homiletical implications of footwear do so at their own peril.

One Saturday evening I drove 200 miles to a small town in Tennessee where I was preaching the next day. On Sunday morning I realized that I brought two left shoes. (I owned two pairs of dress shoes because I once went to preach without any shoes, but that's another story that I should skip.) There are no shoe stores open on Sunday at 8:00 a.m. My first attempt to put a left shoe on my right foot was unbearable. The second shoe, however, was endurable. I could get through it. (It should have been comforting to know that right and left shoes were invented only a little

more than a century ago, but it wasn't.) I considered other options. I could claim to have sprained my ankle and wear one shoe. I could say that I felt preachers should preach on one foot so as to communicate urgency. I could tell the truth.

I was sure that someone was going to ask, "Why are you wearing two left shoes that don't match?" but no one did. I was ready with a response, "Like many Baptists, I was born with two left feet."

When Jesus sent out the 70, he said, "Carry no sandals" (Luke 10:4) — which indicates I should never have had two pairs of dress shoes. This is not a universally helpful suggestion, but God said this to one preacher, "'Go, and loose the sackcloth from your loins and take your sandals off your feet,' and he had done so, walking naked and barefoot" (Isaiah 20:2). On the other hand/foot, the father of the prodigal told the servants, "Put shoes on his feet" (Luke 15:22). John the Baptist said, "I am not worthy to carry his sandals" — which indicates that Jesus wasn't barefoot. Solomon 7:1 exults, "How graceful are your feet in sandals, O queenly maiden!"*

Preachers have to get off on the right foot, because the truth is still putting on its shoes while lies are traveling halfway around the world. Ministers should not be Goody Two-Shoes, but need to walk in the shoes of those to whom they preach. As someone said, "You don't want to dance in a puddle with a hole in your shoe." (This sounds like it might be relevant, but isn't.)

I recently preached at First Baptist Church in Augusta, Ga. The congregation was observing a missions emphasis, so I preached on the sacrifices necessary to be Christ's missionaries. After I finished, Rodger Murchison, the associate pastor, offered the invitation: "Today, we are taking an offering of shoes for our ministry in Liberia. We invite you to come to the front and leave your shoes. I'm about to be barefoot and hope you are, too."

What choice did I have? Like everyone else, I took off my shoes and left them at the front. After the service was over, Rodger graciously offered to let me dig through the pile of shoes to find mine. I was tongue-tied at first, but then said, "That would feel like trading my soul for my soles."

God told Moses, "Remove the sandals from your feet, for the place on which you are standing is holy ground" (Exodus 3:5). I told my student she could preach barefoot. I told myself I should try it, too.

*(Since I wrote a column on shoes, I needed to include a footnote. Solomon 7:1 is not a text on which I would suggest anyone preach.)

Ministry Menu

The most interesting minister in the world
October 2010

Most Baptists claim they do not care for the product, but when we are alone we smile at the commercials featuring "the most interesting man in the world." The advertisements depict a bearded, debonair gentleman in his 50s. While vaguely Spanish music plays in the background, the narrator describes "the most interesting man in the world."

If he punched you in the face, you would have to fight off the strong urge to thank him.

He once taught a German Shepherd to bark in Spanish.

His personality is so magnetic, he is unable to carry credit cards.

He has been known to cure narcolepsy just by walking into a room.

His organ donor card also lists his beard.

He is "the most interesting man in the world."

Each commercial ends with a signature sign-off: "Stay thirsty, my friends."

I am guessing that you and I have exactly the same reaction: Someone needs to make commercials about "the most interesting minister in the world."

When the most interesting minister leads a silent prayer, birds stop singing.

When the most interesting minister prays before the offering is collected, the plates fill with credit cards, earrings and gold watches.

Other ministers have to lead the prayer of confession, because the most interesting minister has nothing to say.

During hymns, the congregation wishes the most interesting minister's lapel mic was on.

When the most interesting minister reads scripture, most assume she wrote it.

When the most interesting minister has a baby dedication, the baby always cries — when he hands the baby back to the mother.

When the most interesting minister leads the children's sermon, everyone comes to the front.

When the most interesting minister steps into the baptistery, the water parts.

When the most interesting minister serves communion, it does not taste like grape juice.

When the most interesting minister preaches, cell phones refuse to ring.

The most interesting minister speaks fluent Hebrew and Greek, but never does so in the pulpit.

Nine months after the most interesting minister's sermon on Song of Solomon, the nursery ran out of space.

When the most interesting minister preached on the Book of Revelation, it made sense.

When the most interesting minister preached on the war in Afghanistan, abortion and gay marriage, everyone agreed with everything she said.

The most interesting minister quotes "The Lighter Side."

The most interesting minister never preaches long enough.

Ministers from other churches join the most interesting minister's church just to shake his hand.

After Sunday services, the most interesting minister autographs orders of worship — which have been known to show up on e-Bay.

When the organ is broken, the most interesting minister fixes it — without tools.

When the most interesting minister speaks at deacons' meetings, deacons repent.

The most interesting minister does not go to committee meetings; they come to him.

The youth have a Sunday for the most interesting minister.

When the most interesting minister served at the Wednesday night supper, the kitchen got a five-star rating in the next day's newspaper.

When the most interesting minister led a Bible study on Genesis 3, apple sales plummeted.

When the most interesting minister performs a wedding ceremony, no one looks at the bride.

When the most interesting minister preaches at a funeral, people cry because the deceased did not get to hear it.

The most interesting minister performs the Christmas pageant as a one-person play.

When the most interesting minister built a house for Habitat for Humanity, it was immediately renamed Habitat for Divinity.

Billy Graham comes to the most interesting minister's crusades.

Joel Osteen copied the most interesting minister's smile.

The most interesting minister knows your name, your birthday and the year of your birth — which she never mentions.

The most interesting minister has been to Israel many times, and each time, peace breaks out.

I don't always go to church. But when I do. I prefer my minister. Stay interesting, ministers.

The secret life of preachers
January 2009

There's more going on in your pastor's head than you imagine. On Sunday morning, your minister's thoughts are as busy as a beehive, spaghetti junction or Walmart on the day after Christmas. During some worship services it sounds like this inside your preacher's brain:

Mary Ann brought her adorable baby to worship again. I wish she would start crying now instead of during the sermon.

I can never sing this hymn without thinking, "On a hill far away stood an old Chevrolet." It's fun to sing this one like Bob Dylan.

It's always interesting when the youth minister prays. I wonder what the record is for the most times saying "like" and "just" in a single prayer.

When we recite the Lord's Prayer, it sounds like the voice on my GPS.

Why does the offering feel like a Nielsen rating?

When I said the youth could usher I didn't expect suits and ties, but who wears sandals in January? I wish I could wear sandals.

Why don't women wear hats to church anymore?

I should eat breakfast before I get here. Two Krispy Kremes during Sunday school is probably a bad idea.

I see the third grade Sunday school teacher gave out jawbreakers again. I wish I had a jawbreaker.

I thought this part of the sermon would go better. Maybe the sound system isn't working. I should have kept the joke about the priest and the rabbi to myself.

I need to remember to ask Ashley about the note Sam just handed her. Maybe I should ask her right now.

Look at that guy looking at his watch. I'll be so glad when football season is over. I wonder who's playing today. Should ministers pull for the Saints?

I need to put the introduction and conclusion closer together next week.

I'd like to see how John the Baptist would react to a cell phone ringing.

Why did I decide to preach on Jesus' baptism? It really is confusing.

I'm glad my congregation can't tell what I'm thinking when I'm preaching.

Some Sundays, pastors think like air traffic controllers a week after a crash. But on the best Sundays, nothing is more holy than the prayers that fill the preacher's head.

God, they showed up again. If I wasn't the pastor, I'm not sure I would show up every Sunday.

Annie Mae is here if I ever need to be reminded that I'm not the best Christian in the room.

It must take Jim 30 minutes to maneuver his walker from his car to his pew, but he's always here.

I can't believe Sandy made it after the horrible week she had. Her son is an alcoholic and her husband is no help, but she never misses worship.

This room is filled with saints who keep coming to church to give themselves to your grace.

Thank you, God.

Singing was one of your best ideas. "So I'll cherish the old, rugged cross." Cherishing crosses is no easy thing.

God, make your kingdom come and your will be done in this congregation.

Forgive me for ever taking worship for granted. Make me discontented with my apathy and grateful for the love that covers us all.

Thank you, God.

I'm glad the sermon isn't limited to what I know — and that these gracious people understand that. It's easy to see why you love them. Some of them are listening so intently for your word.

I can almost picture the dove and hear you saying, "You are my beloved children with whom I am well pleased."

If I'm going to be a good pastor for these good people, I need to give myself to you again. Thank you, God.

On the best Sundays, God speaks not only through the preacher, but also to the preacher — more than we imagine.

Meditation, contemplation, and picante sauce
April 2006

Several years ago some members of the church of which I was the pastor began a Monday night meditation group. They invited me to come to the first meeting, but I had a conflict. I was reading a book, or something. They kept inviting me until finally I thought, "Meditation isn't my thing, but maybe it's because I haven't given it enough of a try."

The group met in a Sunday school room that didn't look like a Sunday school room. They removed all the chairs and replaced them with rugs. I know this even though the lights were off, because there were about 200 candles burning. A tape of nature sounds was playing — babbling brooks, birds chirping, that sort of stuff.

That night, we were to pray with mantras — speaking the same words over and over as a kind of prayer without thinking. I chose the simplest mantra — "Jesus" ... "Christ." I was to pray "Jesus" when I inhaled and "Christ" when I exhaled.

So I began breathing and praying, "Jesus" ... "Christ." I knew we weren't supposed to think, but a thought crossed my mind. Theologically speaking, shouldn't it be the other way around — inhaling Christ and exhaling Jesus? Or maybe not. I told myself to stop thinking — just breathe. "Jesus." "Christ."

After another minute (or maybe it was less), I thought: "I wonder why Jesus never suggested this. Maybe Jesus thinks this is silly. I can't picture St. Peter preaching at Pentecost, 'Men of Israel, I want you to breathe like this.'"

We meditated for about 30 minutes. I really tried, but by the end I was trying to decide whether to pick up chips or ice cream on the way home. When the leader asked us to share our experiences, an earnest woman said she felt hope being born in her heart. Another person had been surrounded by a bright blue light. A third said he felt himself physically reaching out to touch Jesus. I chose not to share that I had decided on picante sauce and Ruffles.

I had gotten an F in meditation, but I decided to return to the group the next Monday and try again. That week we worked on *lectio divina*. In this form of meditation you say one verse of the Bible again and again.

Mine was "Blessed are the merciful, for they will receive mercy." We were again cautioned against analyzing — even thinking — and I tried, but I just couldn't do it.

I remembered that "the Greek word for blessed is *makarios*. The translations that go with 'happy' are so wrong. What's the word for mercy? Is it *elepmones*, or is that sheep? Why am I so lousy at Greek? Maybe I should have taken more Hebrew. I think I hear Jesus laughing at me in Hebrew. I wonder which is more fattening, chips or ice cream?"

I went to the meditation group a half dozen times and always left feeling like a remedial student. Others were having wonderful, mystical experiences, and I was working on a grocery list.

I still feel bad about my failure at meditation, and I feel bad about thinking of meditation as something you can fail, which it clearly isn't, but I have come up with an obvious conclusion. We need to find our own best ways to accept God's gift of contemplation. Some people grow in their faith more with their eyes open than with their eyes closed. Different people experience God in different ways.

We make a mistake if we separate spirituality from the rest of our lives. Think about what makes you feel alive. You've heard people say, "When I sing I feel alive" or "When I'm with my friends I come to life" or "When I run I feel alive."

Wherever we come alive, that's an area in which we're spiritual — filled with the Spirit. In recent years spirituality has been greatly (and helpfully) influenced by monastic practices — silence and solitude. But for many of us, as much as we need times of silence and contemplation, those may not be the times when we feel most alive, most loved by God. We need to claim whatever moments we are most alive as moments of God's presence.

Church Shopping
September 2008

I thought this would be fun, but now I'm not so sure. For the first time since 1983, I'm — and this phrase shouldn't exist — church shopping.

When I went from being a pastor to being a professor, I also went from parson to prospect. Like many, I started out secretly wishing for another church just like my last church, but that's not going to happen. Now I'm trying to figure out what I'm looking for — and how I'll convince my family when I've found it.

I worry that I will look for things church growth experts say visitors look for. When I was a pastor, I secretly thought: "We want to be the church for people who are serious about church. The ones who ask shallow questions would be better off in another church." Now I'm wondering how superficial I want to be …

- Should I pick a church for frivolous reasons?
- How much do I care about convenient parking?
- Are we looking for smiling greeters who wear name tags with big letters so that we don't have to stare at their chests?
- Will we notice how clean the building is? Is cleanliness really next to godliness?
- Do I want to wear a suit each week or buy Sunday-best Bermuda shorts?
- Will I be put off if Sunday school doesn't start on time? (If I feel strongly about punctuality, I may have to join the senior adults.)
- What do we most want from Sunday school? Is it insightful teaching, a sense of community or Krispy Kremes? Should chairs be set in rows, a circle or traded for bean bags?
- Will the sanctuary have comfortable seats?
- Can I deduct a few points if there is a flag?
- Will they choose bad hymns? (Like everyone else, I define these as hymns I don't know.) Should I care if we don't sing the third stanza?
- Will they play inappropriate musical instruments? How unfair is it to believe organs are more sacred than drums?
- How disappointed can I be if all the ushers are male?
- How crazy will it make me when the pastor is younger than I am?

- Can I subtract from their score if the preacher walks around during the sermon?
- What if the minister preaches more than 20 minutes?
- What if the pastor tries to be funny and it doesn't work?
- What if he or she doesn't ask lots of rhetorical questions?
- What if I find it's harder to listen to a sermon than preach one?
- What if the church's idea of ministry is the men's group meeting at the Waffle House on the first Saturday of the month?
- What if former pastors make lousy church members?

I do understand that the churches in the New Testament didn't have parking lots, name tags or buildings. I need to ask better questions:

- Should I choose a church home on the basis of my preferences, or should I look for something more?
- Does the church reflect God's joy?
- Do we feel the presence of the Spirit when we're together?
- Do we welcome those who are left out?
- Does everyone in the church look like me?
- Does the church pray about the war and for the hungry?
- Does the church challenge us to a deeper faith?
- Do we think new thoughts and serve in new ways?
- Do we care for the lost and the poor?
- Can my family help this congregation share the love of God?
- How comfortable should we be?
- Should we be part of a struggling church that demands more than we want to give?
- What church would Jesus join?

Should I have named my son Karl Barth?
October 2008

The earliest I could get an appointment at the seminary housing office was 9:00. I was coming from seven hours away, so I left at 1:30 on Monday morning. I'm fairly certain the good people at student housing would have given me an appointment at 4:00 in the afternoon, but I was too excited to wait. I was as wound up as any new seminary student has ever been wound.

I was pumped to learn Hebrew and Greek backwards and forwards. I planned to read Augustine's *Confessions* in the original Latin. (I didn't mention this to anyone, because I wasn't sure Augustine wrote in Latin.) I intended to pray 30 minutes every morning. I was planning to meet a beautiful, intelligent seminarian. We would get married and name our children Martin Luther and Karl Barth — Martina and Karla if we had girls. I was unreasonably excited for a long time, but then after a while, I calmed down.

The exhilaration gave way to the routine. Hebrew and Greek never quite clicked for me. Augustine's *Confessions* is long. I bought a copy of *Cliff Notes on the New Testament*. When I woke up late I prayed in the car on the way to school. I did marry a beautiful, intelligent seminarian, but we named our children Graham and Caleb — for which they are grateful. I got so used to seminary, I had no desire to leave and stayed seven years. That's not the record.

When I was called to be the pastor of my first church, I was beside myself with excitement. I couldn't believe they were going to pay me to stand up on Sunday and say, "I've been listening carefully, and this is what I think God wants us to hear." It was my job to see hurting people in the world and ask how God might be calling the church to respond. I was going to stir things up and lead my people to take faith more seriously. My church was going to become a beacon for Christ, a shining star for social justice, a guiding light in the evangelical world. All that and I would get a private room at youth camp.

I was unreasonably excited for a long time, but then after awhile, I became more realistic. The exhilaration gave way to the routine. Sundays seemed to roll around every four days. One member fell asleep during every sermon. Deacons meetings weren't all that I had dreamed. When we got stirred up, it usually didn't have anything to do with social justice. I got too old for youth camp food, but I loved being a pastor, so much so that I served as pastor of four churches over 22 years. But on too many days the excitement gave way to reasonableness.

The prospect of teaching at a seminary delights me. On my second day I went to the library and checked out *The Joy of Teaching*. I'm re-reading all of the books I assign. Maybe I'll remember the Hebrew and Greek I've forgotten by osmosis. I love the idea of teaching and learning about Christ's church, studying and sharing the ideas of Christian scholars, and being part of a grace-filled community.

But I am also afraid that the excitement will be overcome by practicality. I fear that when I am trying to share my love for the church I'll remember that "dysfunctional church" can seem redundant. I could skim the books I've read before. I haven't yet read *The Joy of Teaching*, but I've figured out there is no sequel titled *The Joy of Grading*.

It's understandable when we settle into patterns of thinking and acting that are reasonable and expected. But if we don't hold on to some of the imaginative, dream-filled enthusiasm the Spirit sends, we're not following Jesus. God calls us to maintain some level of unreasonable head-over-heels devotion to Christ. God leads us beyond cautious, routine, carefully-measured faith to extravagant possibilities. Every once in a while when we feel the Spirit pulling us to do something new, we should act on the belief that we heard God say, "Go."

The former pastors' club
November 2008

I'm going through withdrawal. I still feel anxious on Saturday night and take a nap on Sunday afternoon — even though I haven't done anything. I seek out former pastors so that we can talk about the glory and gunk of our former lives. Sometimes former pastors get a funny look on their faces as if they're reminiscing about a high school sweetheart who got away. We are Wallendas without a tightrope, Kennedys without politics, Mannings without football. One of the ways I've been dealing with my mixed emotions is compiling a list of things I don't miss about being a pastor.

- I don't miss knowing the party will get louder after I walk out the door.
- I don't miss the alarm going off at 6:45 on Sunday morning.
- I don't miss the phrase, "Pardon my language, Reverend."
- I don't miss there being an 80 percent chance I'll be called on to pray before a meal.
- I don't miss feeling responsible when it rains at the church picnic.
- I don't miss visiting a member's third cousin in the hospital after a knee replacement, because the member "can't get by to see her myself" and seeing the look on the patient's face that says, "Who are you and why are you here?"
- I don't miss business meetings.
- I don't miss saying things like, "I understand that 'You Sexy Thing' is 'your song,' but I think it would be more fitting at the reception than as the processional."
- I don't miss church members thinking I need the latest book by Joel Osteen.
- I don't miss deacons' meetings where Jesus isn't mentioned or wishes he hadn't been mentioned.

Reading my list of things I don't miss about being a pastor might lead you to think I'm feeling only joy about leaving my former occupation, but the list of things I miss is much longer.

- I miss deacons' meetings where deacons speak honestly about how to be the presence of Christ.
- I miss church members thinking I need the latest book by Frederick Buechner.
- I miss worship committee meetings.
- I miss being called "Brother Brett."
- I miss free parking at the hospital.
- I miss having an assistant whose job is to make me look better.
- I miss being given fresh vegetables.
- I miss people insisting on paying for my lunch.
- I miss getting a stack of birthday cards.
- I miss knowing that no matter what I write for the church newsletter, someone kind will say it was good — even if it wasn't.
- I miss hearing children singing, pianos playing and choirs rehearsing.
- I miss bragging about my church.
- I miss sitting at the front during worship. I didn't realize it's the best place to hear the choir.
- I miss deciding which hymns we'll sing.
- I miss reading the Bible aloud and saying, "This is the Word of the Lord."
- I miss serving Communion.
- I miss baptizing young Christians.
- I miss welcoming new members into the church.
- I miss 7-year-olds hugging me because I'm their pastor.
- I miss senior citizens asking me to pray with them.
- I miss knowing homeless people by name, and being known by name.
- I miss the sacred gift of being invited to share the suffering of broken-hearted friends.
- I miss the saints who called me their pastor.

The world's best temp job
March 2010

I was a pastor for 22 years, then (while working weekdays as a professor) a guest preacher for a year and a half, and now — thanks to the gracious people at First Baptist Church, Dalton, Ga. — I am an interim pastor. My friends have suggested I am working my way up the ecclesiastical ladder. I am learning that the differences in these three jobs are subtle, but significant.

For instance, pastors have file cabinets filled with years of sermons. Interims have a set of sermons for each season of the church year. Guest preachers have a file marked "Sermon."

Pastors work hard to plan the worship service. Interims try to fit what the staff has planned. Guest preachers try to remember to e-mail their sermon title.

Pastors rotate their Sunday best. Interims have a couple of choices. Guest preachers go to the cleaners every four churches.

Pastors fill in when Sunday school teachers call in sick. Interims go to Sunday school assemblies to get a donut. Guest preachers get to church halfway through Sunday school.

Pastors have their own parking spot. Interims try to avoid parking in someone else's spot. Guest preachers park across the street.

Pastors know all the children's names. Interims know the staff's children. Guest preachers wish the children would be quiet during the sermon.

Pastors try to make improvements between the 8:30 and the 11:00 service. Interims show off the names they have learned. Guest preachers look for coffee.

Pastors know who not to hug. Interims hug everyone who looks like they might want to be hugged. Guest preachers shake hands.

Pastors pay when they go out to eat. Interims never pick up a check. Guest preachers order off the dollar menu at the drive-thru.

Pastors try to keep things moving in the right direction during deacons' meetings. Interims sit in the back. Guest preachers watch television.

Pastors go to the hospital each Monday. Interims go to the hospital when a deacon is ill. Guest preachers do not know where the hospital is.

Pastors worry about the church's budget. Interims tell the church to worry about the church budget. Guest preachers forget that churches have budgets.

Pastors go on mission trips to underprivileged areas. Interims praise church members who go on mission trips to underprivileged areas. Guest preachers go to Florida.

Pastors find that Holy Week is the busiest time of the year. Interims feel like they are pastors again at Easter. Guest preachers don't have an Easter sermon.

Pastors' families feel like everyone is watching. Interims introduce their families at Easter. Guest preachers call their spouse on the way home.

Pastors think they have to fix mistakes the last pastor made. Interims try to fix problems before the next pastor arrives. Guest preachers make jokes about the pastor being at the beach.

Pastors have messy offices. Interims have several books on the shelf. Guest preachers have the aforementioned file marked "Sermon."

When I was growing up, evangelists offered invitations to "full-time Christian service." It sounded right. "Part-time Christian service" does not seem like much of a commitment. Now I am not so sure. Maybe there is something to be said for "part-time Christian service." Being an interim seems like fun.

Pastors, interims and guest preachers have different jobs, but they all have the joy and responsibility of standing before God's people and saying, "I've been listening for God's word and this is what I think I heard God say."

Holiday Staples

Dear Advent Expert

December 2003

As the pastor of a church with liturgical worship, you might guess that I get questions from young ministers concerning Advent. I don't but if I did, they might read like this:

> *Pastor, Liturgical Baptist Church:*
> *What's the deal with Advent?*
> *A Young Minister*

> *Young Minister:*
> *The word Advent comes from the Latin advenire, which means "coming." The Advent season (which includes the four Sundays prior to Christmas) focuses on the coming of God in the past, present and future.*
> *Your Guide to Advent*

> *Mr. Liturgy:*
> *The deacons got into an argument over which candle to light on the Second Sunday of Advent. We have three yellows and two greens left.*
> *Liturgically Challenged*

> *Rev. L.C.:*
> *Light whatever works for you, but a traditional approach is to use three purple candles and one pink for the Third Sunday.*
> *Keeping the Candles Burning*

> *Adventurer:*
> *Advent is going great. Almost everyone loves it. In fact, we even have a sign out in front of the church that says "14 Shopping Days Left in Advent."*
> *Counting Days*

Shopping Liturgist:

I'm delighted that Advent is going so well. You might want to talk about the differences between the commercial aspects of Christmas — shopping, decorating, baking and socializing — and Advent— which is meant to move our attention toward God's presence.

Also Shopping

Dr. Advent:

Who started Advent? I've got a 10 spot riding on the Seventh Day Adventists.

Needing Money for Gifts

Gambler:

Pope Gregory I (590-604)) instituted the four-week Advent celebration. Don't make any more wagers. Advent shouldn't be about losing money.

Grateful to Gregory

Father Christmas:

I have been following the scriptures for Advent and am disappointed. The texts deal with judgment and repentance. Why is Advent such a downer? Why can't we read about Christmas?

Wondering

Wonderer:

I'm not sure "downer" is fair, but you have a point. It's Pope Sylvester II's fault. Before his reign (999-1003) in France and Germany, Advent was spent fasting in preparation for the Last Judgment (especially as they neared the year 1000). Meanwhile, the church in Italy celebrated four weeks of parties leading up to the Feast of the Nativity. Because the French and Germans had more influence, Sylvester went with their less joyful Advent. Through the years the penitential approach became the focus of the entire church. I'm with you. There's a lot to be said for an Italian Advent.

Wishing You a Roman Holiday

Italian-at-heart Friend:
We got into another argument at the last deacons meeting. We know that the Advent themes include hope, peace and love, but is the fourth theme forbearance, self-control or self-esteem?
Guessing It's Forbearing

Forbearing One:
You're talking about a recent innovation. It's hope, peace, joy and love, but self-control is good, too.
Joyfully

Self-appointed Expert:
Everyone but Mrs. Wendleken is on board with Advent. During the lighting of the candles she mutters under her breath, "Advent Shmadvent."
What to do?

Advent Friend:
You could say, "Mrs. Wendleken, people who are not as spiritual as you need to be reminded of the presence of God" — or you could leave a lump of coal in her Advent stocking. Merry Advent,
Brett

Christmas Quiz
December 2009

Most readers of *Baptists Today* have an extensive, inconclusive and superfluous knowledge of the Christmas stories in the Gospels. Scholars argue that we should not try to reconcile the stories in Matthew and Luke, but scholars are not always the most fun at the Christmas party. While no prizes will be awarded — only in part because the answers are provided — this could start you on your way to yuletide joy.

_____ 1. The Roman emperor at the birth of Christ was: a. Quirinius. b. Julius Caesar. c. Julius Caesar's nephew. d. deceased by the time Jesus was born.

_____ 2. There was snow that first Christmas: a. all over Israel. b. somewhere in Israel. c. nowhere in Israel. d. for the very first time in history.

_____ 3. According to Luke, who did Mary first visit with the news of Jesus? a. Anna. b. Joseph. c. Elizabeth. d. Dr. Luke.

_____ 4. Also according to Luke, how did Mary and Joseph make the trip from Nazareth to Bethlehem? a. on camel. b. Joseph walked; Mary rode the donkey. c. Mary walked; Joseph rode the donkey. d. Luke doesn't say. e. in silence; Mary wasn't real thrilled with the timing of the trip.

_____ 5. Which are the innkeeper's recorded words? a. "There's no room." b. "I have a stable." c. "Come back after the Christmas rush." d. none of the above.

_____ 6. When Jesus was born, Mary and Joseph were: a. dating. b. betrothed. c. married. d. not speaking.

_____ 7. The baby Jesus cried: a. like other babies. b. at the little drummer boy's song. c. he never cried, but he would not be thrilled with this quiz.

_____ 8. A manger is a: a. cradle. b. trough. c. stable. d. any vehicle in which you get "away."

_____ 9. Which animals does the Bible mention as being present at Jesus' birth? a. cows, sheep, goats. b. only sheep. c. lions and tigers and bears. d. none.

_____ 10. What "sign" did the angels tell the shepherds to look for? a. "This way to baby Jesus." b. a star. c. a baby in a manger. d. a baby that doesn't cry.

_____ 11. What did the angels sing? a. "Joy to the World." b. "Glory to God in the Highest." c. "Unto Us a Child Is Born." d. the song about chestnuts.

(Isn't this great? Do you think you've missed any yet? You've looked at the answers, haven't you? You don't have the Christmas spirit at all, do you?)

_____ 12. What does Magi mean? a. wise ones. b. kings. c. any person in the Christmas play wearing a bathrobe.

_____ 13. What is myrrh? a. an easily shaped metal. b. a spice used for burying people. c. a drink. d. According to recent New Testament scholarship, myrrh and frankincense are the same thing.

_____ 14. As long as Christmas has been celebrated, it has been on Dec. 25th. (true or false)

_____ 15. This quiz was: a. a time of thoughtful biblical inquiry that helped prepare me for this Christmas season in a new and fascinating way. b. well worth the time. c. about 15 questions too long.

(You're not supposed to look at these until you finish.)
1. c. Luke 2:1
2. b. Mount Hermon in Israel is always snow covered.
3. c. Luke 1:39
4. d. Some have argued that a carpenter wouldn't own a donkey.
5. d. The innkeeper isn't mentioned.
6. b. Luke 2:5. This doesn't get mentioned much in some churches..
7. a. like other babies.
8. b. "Manger" is from the French word for eating.
9. d. The Hallmark Cards people don't let it bother them.
10. c. Luke 2:12
11. b. Luke 2:14
12. a. They were trained in astrology and dream interpretation.
13. b. The spice serves an aromatic purpose.
14. False. It wasn't until the fourth century that Dec. 25th was celebrated.
15. Don't be a grinch.

In with the old, in with the new
January 2011

Why isn't January's namesake featured on more church newsletters and websites? Janus, the Roman god of beginnings, endings and time, has two heads that face opposite directions. One head looks back at the last year while the other looks forward to the new, simultaneously looking into the future and the past. Janus would be a fine symbol for congregations that cannot decide which direction they should be facing. The absolute necessity of both old and new is obvious, and yet old and new have a longstanding, ongoing battle in the church.

We have been to churches that hope tomorrow will be 1958 and churches that stay away from anything older than they are; churches that still give 10 points for reading the Bible every day and 20 for being on time and churches that discuss the theological implications of the films of Will Ferrell; churches that got their Hammond organ when the funeral home closed and churches that got their drums when the pastor's rock band broke up; churches that smell of incense and churches that smell like the gymnasiums they are six days of the week; churches with paintings of rivers in the baptistery and churches where the baptistery is a river; churches where they hug and say, "God loves you and I do, too" and churches where no one has hugged in years; churches with kneeling, reciting and genuflecting and churches with clapping, waving and dancing; churches that are emerging and churches that are submerging; churches that love whatever is covered with dust and churches enamored with whatever came in the mail this morning.

The churches in which I grew up loved the old. Things seldom changed. One churchgoer put it this way: "This is what I learned at First Baptist Church. I learned that unleavened bread is Chicklet-sized soda crackers. I learned that the Hebrew word for grape juice is spelled w-i-n-e. I learned that the moneychangers at the temple were communists, not capitalists. I learned that every passage of scripture has three points."

We were serious about the ancient words. We had dog-eared Bibles with multi-colored underlining and sermon notes scribbled in the margin. We taped memory verses to our mirrors, refrigerators and baby beds. We took sin seriously. The church warned us about the dangers of worldliness and the hypnotic glitter of having, doing and thinking what the sinful crowd has, does and thinks.

There are so many good things about churches that love the old that it takes a while to realize that some crucial things are missing. God calls us in new, surprising ways. Churches in love with the old miss the gospel that's always new.

There is also danger in the opposite direction. Some churches accept only what's new and push aside everything that's old. We've been to churches that love the new. They can be a lot of fun. It's fun to sing without a hymnal when the words are on a big, big screen. It's fun to hear easily understood, often alliterative sermons with titles such as, "How to Be Happy," "How to Have a Happy Marriage," "How to Have Happy Children" and "How to Have Happy Children Who Will Have Happy Marriages." It's fun to watch clips from *Avatar* that supposedly illuminate the story of David and Goliath. It's fun to have Pepsi and potato chips for the Lord's Supper. It's fun to go to church and be surprised by what's new.

Churches that love only the new can be so much fun, so genuinely joyful, that it takes a while to realize something is missing. God calls us to walk ancient paths. Churches in love with the new miss the old gospel.

Jesus' advice is to love the best of the old and the new: "Every scribe who has been trained for the kingdom of heaven is like a householder who brings out of the treasury what is new and what is old" (Matt. 13:52). We know it is not either/or, but both/and. We read the new by an old light. We see the old in a light that is new each day. Janus had the right idea. We need to look both ways.

Groundhog Day, Holy Day
February 2007

The true measure of a family isn't how they celebrate Thanksgiving or Christmas. Everyone knows how to eat turkey and decorate a tree. The real test is Groundhog Day.

Every year for the last 13, our family has gathered on Feb. 2 to watch the romantic comedy *Groundhog Day*. Bill Murray plays a self-centered Pittsburgh weatherman covering the Groundhog Day Festival in Punxsutawney. To his astonishment, Phil finds himself trapped living his least favorite day of the year over and over. This combination of *It's a Wonderful Life* and *The Twilight Zone* may not seem like the most heartwarming tradition, but after 13 viewings, our family will be quoting lines in unison.

"This is one time when television really fails to capture the true excitement of a large squirrel predicting the weather."

"There's a major network interested in me."

"That would be the Home Shopping Network."

"Do you ever have déjà vu, Mrs. Lancaster?"

"I don't think so, but I could check with the kitchen."

"I'll give you a weather prediction. It's gonna be cold, it's gonna be gray, and it's gonna last the rest of your life."

"Have you ever had déjà vu?"

Illustration by Scott Brooks

"Didn't you just ask me that?"

"What would you do if you were stuck in one place and every day was exactly the same and nothing you did ever mattered?"

"That about sums it up for me."

As is often the case, the silly and the sacred aren't far apart. Phil finally figures out that the only thing he can change is himself. If he is to win the heart of a kind woman, he will have to become kind. The questions posed by Phil's predicament are spiritual.

What would it take to make an ordinary day into the best day of your life? If you were trying to convey your love to a genuinely caring person, what might you change about yourself? How do we break out of living the same day over and over?

Like Thanksgiving and Christmas, too many people don't appreciate the sacred beginnings of Groundhog Day. This holy day began — and I'm not telling you anything you don't already know — with Candlemas. This festival, which Christians started celebrating in the fourth century, commemorates the presentation of Jesus in the temple 40 days after his birth (Feb. 2). When the prophet Simeon saw the baby he said, "Mine eyes have seen your salvation … a light for revelation." For more than 1,500 years the followers of Jesus have been lighting candles on Feb. 2 to symbolize Jesus coming as the light of the world.

The groundhog portion of the tradition — if he sees his shadow, winter is six weeks from ending — is founded on an old Scottish couplet:

If Candlesmas Day is bright and clear,
There'll be two winters in the year.

So on Feb. 2, wish everyone "Happy Candlemas," write a Groundhog Day carol (my son Graham did this once, but asked me not to mention it), pretend your sausage biscuit is groundhog, quote some Scottish poetry, take a candle to your church and ask your pastor to bless it (like they do in Germany), eat crêpes (like the French do, but only after 8:00 p.m.), cancel your boat trip (like superstitious sailors do), watch a movie (like the Youngers), or just thank God for the light that helps us see the silly and sacred gifts that are new each day.

Dear Lent Expert
March 2007

As the pastor of a church with liturgical worship and pretentious staff members, you might guess that I get questions from young ministers concerning Lent. I don't but if I did, they might read like this:

> Pastor, High Church Baptist Church:
> What's the deal with Lent?
> *A Young Minister*

> Young Minister:
> Lent, a tradition that may go back as far as the fifth century, is the 40-day period before Easter, excluding Sundays. It begins on Ash Wednesday and ends on Holy Saturday. If you take Lent seriously, it can seem longer.
> *Father Lent*

> Mr. Liturgy:
> Why don't Sundays count as part of the 40 days?
> *Liturgically Challenged*

> L.C:
> Lent is a time of confession and repentance, but because Sunday is the day on which Christ arose, it's always a party day (as anyone who goes to a Baptist church knows).
> *Sunday Party Planner*

> Lentmeister:
> What are your memories of Lent growing up?
> *Lent Lover*

> Sentimental Lentenist:
> I believe that G.A. Coronation Night — the biggest event of the year — may have fallen during Lent. (If you aren't over 40 or didn't grow up Baptist, it's hard to explain.)
> *46 and Counting*

Rev. Lent:
    Why are the 40 days called "Lent"?
                                                              Trying to Stump You

Not Going to Happen:
    Lent is the Old English word for spring. You could argue that Lent is spring cleaning for the soul, but it is more likely a reference to the season of the year in which Lent falls.
                                                    Already Simmering in Texas

Brother Lent:
    Why do people give up something for Lent?
                                                      Thinking about Chocolate

Dear Cocoa:
    When you skip a meal or alter your routine, you are trying to remember, if not always successfully, Jesus' sacrificial life and death. In theory, by giving up good things we free ourselves from dependence on them, cultivate the spiritual discipline of sacrifice and remind ourselves of the importance of the spiritual over the material. In practice, I know several people I'll avoid if they give up coffee.
                                                      Caffeinated Clergyman

Dr. Lent:
    What do you suggest giving up for Lent?
                                                     Considering Cauliflower

Carnivore:
    The most common practice is to fast for certain days in Lent. Not eating doesn't make some of us more spiritual. Think about giving up television, newspapers, eating out or shopping. Use the time or money you save on something you can imagine Jesus spending the time or money on.
                                                      Still Eating Greens

Self-appointed Expert:
   What are you giving up for Lent?
                              Self-appointed Inquisitor

Self:
   I'm planning to add something for Lent. Instead of reading the sports section each day, I'm going to spend each day with a psalm. (During March Madness I may cheat and read both.) Treat Lent as time set aside to do whatever is necessary to be honest to God about your life. If we stop pursuing pleasure, then, come Easter, we might be caught by joy.
                              Praying for Resurrection

Pomp and circumstances
May 2011

For the next few weeks people with last names like mine will be wondering why alphabetical order is so popular. We are about to begin graduation season. Ivy League schools will have ex-presidents, Nobel laureates and European heads of state giving their graduation speeches. Major college football powers get billionaires, TV anchors and *American Idol* winners. Baptist colleges get unknown novelists, retired astronauts and Baptist preachers.

Commencement speakers try to say something memorable. Graduates hear that there is happiness waiting for them and there is danger waiting for them. They need to embrace the old values and throw out the old values. The world needs more poets and dreamers, and the world does not need any more poets and dreamers.

If you have a high school graduation on your calendar and have not been to one lately, brace yourself. You may be surprised to see a sign over the entrance that says, "No noisemakers. No balloons." You may naïvely think, "That's unnecessary. No one would bring noisemakers or balloons to a solemn ceremony like graduation." You will be wrong. The metal detector will also be a clue that this is not your father's graduation.

The gym, which is normally the home for less rowdy events such as basketball games, will be filled with signs celebrating Victoria, Teddy, Luz,

Doogie, Little Jelly and a host of other 18-year-olds. Try not to sit behind someone with a banner. The students, even the ones wearing sunglasses indoors at 8:00 at night, will be better behaved than the parents who scream through the choir's anthem.

The person seated directly behind you will have a special talent for ear-piercing whistling. This is a skill he loves to share. Someone you will wish ill will bring a plastic clapper — which is even more irritating than the air horns and cowbells. You will imagine how bad it would have been if they had allowed noisemakers.

As the graduates' names are called, spectators will shriek, screech and squeal as though they are shocked to hear their loved one's name called, as though their child is the next contestant on *The Price Is Right*.

It will not be a bad graduation, but it may not be exactly what you would have chosen. At the last few graduations I have attended I felt like an old man. Back in my day there were more men in suits and ties than baseball caps and earrings. We waited quietly for the first strains of "Pomp and Circumstance." The students acted as though they were not surprised to have graduated.

We listened solemnly as the speaker droned on about how the word commencement means to begin and so this is not the end of something but the beginning of a lifelong journey, a time of marching to the beat of our own drummers, taking the road less traveled, lighting candles rather than cursing the darkness, and following our hearts. We applauded politely at the end. The ceremony was dignified, serious and meaningful in its way. Shouting may be a fun way to celebrate a graduation, but it is not the way some of us best experience important rites of passage.

In a couple of weeks my son Graham will graduate from Davidson College. My guess is that it will be a fine ceremony — less serious than I might choose and less jubilant than Graham might want. While I am sitting quietly giving thanks for the end of this season of tuition bills — Caleb is a high school junior, call if you have an extra scholarship — I hope I will remember that solemnity and joyfulness are both good gifts of God.

Churches have almost come to blows over whether God is better heard in an organ or a guitar. Sometimes, worship is fast and loud — a fine way to celebrate God's goodness. At other times, worship is solemn and thoughtful — also a fine way to celebrate God's goodness. Some of us feel like God whispers more than God shouts. Maybe that is worth shouting about.

Why Baptists should do Pentecost
June 2011

When I was growing up Baptist, the biggest church days were Mother's Day, Easter and G.A. Coronation (imagine a royal wedding where Jesus is mentioned constantly). Pentecost was not on the list. We may have skipped Pentecost because my kind of Baptists were a little uncomfortable with the spookiest member of the Trinity. The Holy Spirit was a theologically suspect Caspar the Friendly Ghost. When we saw a sign that said "Holy Ghost Revival," we were nervous about what was going on inside.

Some Baptists are still uneasy with snakes, dancing and the banjo music occasionally associated with the Spirit. If *TV Guide* lists "The Holy Spirit Hour" on the Trinity Broadcast Network, channel 345, at 1 a.m., we do not expect Bill Moyers to be the host. The hour is more likely to feature a singing, shouting evangelist with gravity-defying hair slapping people on the forehead while asking for money to pay for his mansion in the Bahamas.

Pentecost's color scheme may be a problem. Christians in liturgical churches often wear bright red on Pentecost. Some Baptists do not look good in red. Johnny Cash was never the man in scarlet. Most find it hard to picture Billy Graham in a cherry suit. (Carrie Underwood is an exception — a Baptist who looks good in red.)

The word "Pentecost" may sound too much like "Pentecostal" for some Baptists. The Baptists who moved into town looked down on

This is not a Baptist preacher

the Pentecostals like the Methodists looked down on the Baptists. The Presbyterians looked down on the Methodists. The Episcopalians looked down on the Presbyterians. The Pentecostals thought the Episcopalians were in dire need of some Pentecost.

The Pentecost story itself includes another complication. Peter's sermon begins with a line for which my Baptist mother does not care. Imagine your pastor opening with, "I know what you are thinking, but in spite of the way they look and the sounds you have been hearing, the choir is not drunk. I can assure you that the choir is not drunk, because it is only 11 o'clock in the morning."

We should ignore that part and listen to the story again. At the end of chapter 1 of the Book of Acts, the disciples are getting organized. They choose a new person to fill the vacancy Judas left on the board. They select Matthias by throwing dice — which would usually be a fine way for a church to choose deacons, but in this instance leads to a forgettable choice.

The disciples talk about how best to go about the business of incorporating as a 501(c)3 organization. Peter begins his Power Point presentation: "Listen carefully. Here are three keys to an effective organization: #1. competent programs, #2. solid financial resource, #3. adequate facilities and parking."

Peter is fiddling with the remote when pandemonium breaks out. Nothing about the preparations they have been making prepares them for what happens. Whatever they thought was coming next turns out to be wrong. Everything comes loose. The Spirit blows their agenda away. Women hang on to their shawls. Men pull on their coats. The wind sounds like a freight train. Something like fire dances on each person's face. The storm and the flames push them out of the fellowship hall and into the street. People who have never been to a church business meeting are suddenly in the middle of a doozy.

No one is sure what is happening with the wind, fire and foreign languages. Some jump to the aforementioned peculiar conclusion, though in the midst of chaos, it is not surprising that they thought they smelled another kind of spirit.

God breathes life into the church with a mighty rush of wind because nothing less would do. When they sing "Just As I Am" 3,000 walk the aisle. That sounds Baptist.

So, on Pentecost, wear red. Light candles. Turn on the fans. Sing. Shout. Dance. Celebrate the Spirit.

Giving thanks in a world of greed
November 1997

When my father asked if he could take our children to buy a board game, I reacted like any alert 1990s parent. I gave him a list of elements that were off-limits: dungeons, dragons, knives, guns, grenades, GI Joe and GI Jane.

My father raised a gentle protest, but he agreed to abide by our "silly" guidelines. Despite my politically correct directions, my father came back with a game more violent and frightening than anything I had imagined.

He bought Monopoly.

The initial contest brought out all the greed I had feared my parents and children possessed — but had never seen completely unrestrained. Acting morally superior, I refused to play, but I hovered nearby to offer alternate interpretations.

Early on, Caleb, our 4-year-old, bought North Carolina and Pacific avenues. When his grandma bought Pennsylvania, spoiling his monopoly bid, he burst into hysterics. I tried to explain that in our far-too-transient society, it would be nice to have extended family living nearby, but he remained upset.

I encouraged Graham, our 9-year-old, to put a house on Baltic Avenue and invest in the community, but he selfishly insisted on locating in a pricier, yellow neighborhood.

When Grandma got a phone call, I agreed to sit in for a couple of turns, believing that I could be a voice for community renewed.

I announced that I would be giving some of Grandma's money to her husband and grandchildren. Grandpa and Caleb were horrified initially. They were certain there had to be a rule against such behavior. Graham suggested, however, that Grandma might want to give the gift of real estate.

The object of Monopoly should raise eyebrows. The goal is to build a fortune by bankrupting your neighbors.

The rules are questionable at best. For instance, the income tax is 10 percent or $200 — whichever is less. The more money you have, the smaller percentage you pay.

The poor tax, meanwhile, is $15. Doesn't that seem low? Doesn't the luxury tax, $75, indicate that players have more to give?

There has to be a better way. Can we envision a game in which people work together to make their community better? Could everyone at the table work to put a nice, green house in every neighborhood? Couldn't we be grateful for what we have without coveting someone else's spot on Boardwalk?

The box should carry a parental warning label. At the end of his first, painful game, Caleb announced: "I'm never going to play this again." It wasn't true. He's addicted — like so many people. Most never unlearn the lessons of Monopoly.

Capitalism has shaped our basic assumptions about life and lessened our sense of gratitude. The prevailing belief is that everyone should pursue his or her own self-interest. In so many areas of our lives — social, political and spiritual — selfishness has been enshrined as a primary value.

At Thanksgiving we celebrate pilgrims, Norman Rockwell, football and gluttony. But as a nation, we don't quite get it. We feel sentimental, but we also hold on to what we have and wish for more.

When we live gratefully, we no longer see life at the expense of others. We're not, as America's favorite board game might indicate, self-made people.

We can work for money, success and much of what most people think of as happiness, but the best gifts — joy, grace and hope — can only be received as the gifts of God. We are here to give thanks.

Family Favorites

Why I love butter pecan
August 2006

My life would have been so much less if I had gotten in the line for chocolate. At the Welcome Students Ice Cream Social at Southern Seminary in 1983, a friend pointed out a gorgeous woman in a hideous Mexican dress, "That's Carol Davis. She went to Seventh. Go introduce yourself."

I nervously got in line for butter pecan — which I didn't really care for — because that's the flavor she was scooping. Carol and I both went to Seventh and James Baptist Church in Waco, but never met because she was in the in-crowd. I desperately tried to think of a clever line and decided to go with "The last time I had butter pecan was at Seventh and James." When I got to the front of the line I was so tongue-tied that nothing came out. Carol was merciful and chose not to make fun of me (a pattern we have continued to this day).

On a hunch that such a compassionate woman would be there, I went to the first meeting of Seminarians United Against Hunger. Carol was there, but she was talking to a handsome seminarian whom I felt sure wasn't there out of concern for the hungry.

A week later God sent the break I needed. A group of us decided to go to a movie, but then participants began dropping out one by one until it was just Carol and me. (How could this not be providential?)

I called and tried to sound confident: "Carol, this is Brett ... Brett Younger ... I was your best customer for butter pecan ... Yes, that's me. We're the only two planning to go to the movie on Monday. Are you still willing to go?" (This probably wasn't the best way to phrase the question.)

The movie was *Harold and Maude* (a 19-year-old man and 80-year-old woman fall in love — what a perfect date movie!). I wasn't used to speaking to attractive women, and hoped that if I were quiet she would assume I was thoughtful. Once during the movie I put my arm on the armrest between us.

On Tuesday I gave Carol a dozen roses. On Saturday we went to lunch. On Sunday evening I went to hear Carol preach. After worship we talked about getting married. On Monday we named our first child — Jenna Hope. (When our son Graham was born, we reconsidered.)

Reasonable people would be embarrassed to admit they talked about marriage within a week of their first date, but on Aug. 4 Carol and I will have been married 22 years.

After more than a score of wedded bliss, I can tell you that living with a real Christian can be a real pain. Carol gives away more money than I want to give away. She makes the grudges I want to harbor seem petty. I wear an imaginary "WWCD" (What would Carol do?) bracelet everywhere I go. It's hard to be married to someone who is kinder, smarter and more Christian than you are.

And it's wonderful. To come from and return to a gracious marriage every day is sheer joy. I'm grateful for the love she gives her family, friends, church and the writing that inspires people she'll never meet. Living with Carol makes we want to be kinder, smarter and more Christian. On Aug. 4 I'll have a big scoop of butter pecan and thank God.

Illustration by Scott Brooks

What kind of fiend?
April 2010

When Carol was six months pregnant with our first child, she was scheduled to take a trip to Alabama for a writer's conference.

We asked our doctor repeatedly, "Is it okay for her to take this trip?"

He kept reassuring us, "Yes, this is fine. There's no reason for Carol not to go."

The WMU sent tickets for a 9 a.m. flight out of Louisville, Ky., about an hour from our home in Indiana. We left in plenty of time, but about two miles down the road our little red Subaru died. We coasted into a gas station. I tried to get the car started, but it wasn't going to start. After a while even if it did start, we had spent so much time trying to get it started that it was doubtful we could make the plane.

The cashier at the gas station, who was a member of our church, loaned us her car. We drove as quickly as we could, all the time realizing that we weren't going to make the departure and we didn't. It had started to rain, so traffic was moving slowly. We got to the airport 20 minutes after the plane was to leave. We went to the counter to see what arrangements could be made and were told that the plane had not yet left, "If you run, you might make it."

We moved as fast as an expectant father will let a six-months expectant mother move. It was a harrowing, comical experience.

"Carol, don't run."

"We have to. Catch up now."

At the gate we were told the plane would not be leaving for 30 minutes. There was a big storm in Alabama that they were hoping would clear. We sat down to catch our breath. The plane was not the big jet we were expecting, but a twin-engine prop plane — a small one. The light rain was heavy when they finally started to board.

Carol turned to me and said, "If you don't want me to go, then I don't have to."

Looking at the plane and the rain, I came close, but then, just like Bogie, I said, "If you don't go, you'll regret it — maybe not today or tomorrow, but someday, and for the rest of your life."

They had trouble getting the plane started. As it finally taxied off, I thought I spotted a funnel cloud. The drizzle was a downpour, and our umbrella was in our car at the gas station. In my hurry I had failed to note carefully what kind of car I had borrowed. I thought it might be blue. The keys said "Ford," and I felt reasonably sure that it would have Indiana license plates. I ran through the rain in a remarkably large airport parking lot, looking for a Ford from Indiana that might be blue that my key would open.

After trying to open enough doors to look like a really poor car thief and after a period of time that seemed infinitely longer than it actually was, I stumbled on to the right car. I drove home in a thunderstorm and passed the time worrying about Carol. I finally got home and waited for her to call. I knew when she was originally supposed to get there. That time passed. I knew when the delay should have put her there. That time passed. I decided on a reasonable time at which to start seriously worrying. That time passed. I couldn't get the picture out of my mind of her offering not to go. Now I could see that she was practically begging not to go.

What kind of fiend forces a pregnant woman on to a crop duster in a tornado? The phone rang. My heart raced. I was rude to someone who wasn't Carol. Then it rang again, and this time I heard her voice calling my name, telling me that everything was okay.

I think about that day every Easter when I read the resurrection story in John. Jesus turns to Mary and calls her name. In that one word, in the calling of her name, joy overwhelms despair.

Mary was convinced of the resurrection not when she saw the empty tomb or even Jesus himself, but when she heard Christ say her name. Easter is the opportunity to hear God calling our names, letting us know that, in spite of our fears, everything is going to be okay.

Caleb's credit card
April 2001

Aug. 17, 2000

President, First USA Bank
Wilmington, DE 19885-5922

To Whom It May Concern:

I am writing this letter for my son Caleb. (I have a hard time getting him to write thank-you notes, much less a formal letter to a big credit card company executive.) Thank you for your recent offer. I'm embarrassed to admit that I opened your letter, which was clearly addressed to Caleb, by mistake. When I saw the Platinum MasterCard return address, I foolishly assumed that it was for me rather than my 6-year-old.

Caleb was surprised that you offered him a "Credit Line Up to $100,000" — more than the credit lines of many of his fellow first graders. Caleb's allowance is $3 a week, so a $100,000 credit line would provide him with substantially more financial flexibility. Caleb has begun noticing which stores take MasterCard. McDonald's, the sno-cone place, putt-putt and the bowling alley don't take your card, but Barnes and Noble, Toys 'R' Us and On the Border (his favorite restaurant — he likes the beeper) do.

At first I was somewhat perplexed by your offer. I even thought about suggesting that you rethink your policy of offering credit cards to people who can't yet ride the roller coasters at Six Flags until I saw that your offer was for a "Select" Platinum MasterCard. I can only assume that Caleb has been "selected" through a careful screening process. Caleb is, as I'm sure you know, very good at math. He can multiply up to fives, though his division is shaky. Caleb is extremely responsible with his money. The dollar bills come out of his piggy bank slowly, if at all. If I were going to give access to $100,000 to anyone whose favorite television show is *Bugs Bunny*, Caleb would be at the top of my list, too.

We have thoughtfully weighed the advantages and disadvantages of your offer. Caleb was pleased with the introductory 2.9% fixed APR for up to nine months, but a little concerned about the 15.4% APR that kicks in after that. Your "exceptional platinum benefits" are impressive, but some

75

would be of little value to Caleb. "Auto rental insurance," for instance, is superfluous as most major rental car companies shortsightedly choose not to rent to people under four feet tall. The $3,000 lost luggage insurance is, however, extremely attractive. Every time we visit his grandparents, Caleb loses something.

In looking at the application form, Caleb wondered if his lack of a business telephone number or employer as well as his inability to sign his name in cursive would disqualify him, but I pointed out that he has no monthly house payment, a spotless credit history, and that decent people don't offer you something unless they plan to give it to you.

I have been thinking about the significance of you offering my child such a magnificent credit card 10 years before he's eligible for a driver's license. I doubt that anybody needs a $100,000 credit line, but it seems especially too much too soon for someone who considers Pez a major food group.

After lengthy conversation, careful consideration and intense soul-searching, Caleb has decided that, for now at least, he will not be taking advantage of your generous offer. Your slogan "It's all the card you need —and more" is especially fitting for Caleb — particularly the "and more."

Please do not take his decision as a reflection on your "quality, heritage, and high level of customer service." If Caleb were going to get a credit card with a credit line of $100,000 it would be yours.

Sincerely,
Rev. Brett Younger

P.S. If I end up having to renegotiate his allowance, it's your fault.

***

Sept. 15, 2000

Re: Future Cardmember Caleb Younger

Dear Reverend Younger:

Thank you for taking the time to write us on behalf of Caleb. We would also like to thank him for taking the time out of his busy schedule of appointments with Bugs and multiplication lessons to consider our offer.

We were pleased to hear that he was impressed with the benefits of the Platinum Card. We anxiously await some time in 2012 when we will receive his application to process.

Until that time, we have removed his name from our mailing list. Please let him know that we have not forgotten him, but do not want to bother him with any other offer right now. After all, his schedule sounds very full.

We would like to congratulate Caleb on such a wonderful job saving his allowance. Please let him know that when he needs more credit than his piggy can offer, we would be honored to have him as our card member.

We really appreciated hearing from you. Your letter brought a smile to my face. I hope the enclosed contribution brings a smile to his. Maybe he can buy some Pez and have some left over for his Piggy!

If you have any other concerns or would like to apply for an account for yourself, please give me a call.

Sincerely,

Meredith Kidd
Office of the President

***

Sept. 21, 2000

Dear Meredith,

I'm sorry we missed you when we called. Caleb sounds fine, but I always get flustered talking to answering machines.

Thank you for all the presents you sent. The day we got your package, Caleb took his family to McDonald's to spend the gift certificates (two twist cones, a hot fudge sundae, an Oreo McFlurry, and a dollar left over). The Minnie Mouse Pez dispenser has already been loaded and unloaded. You were right to go with grape. It took me longer than I would like to admit to figure out that the bubble-blowing pens weren't just pens, but fortunately Caleb's mother has seen such exotic gifts before. We've yo-yoed with the Bank One yo-yo and written with the Bank One pencils. One eye on the fish pen has fallen off, but such is life. The dollar bill is in Caleb's piggy bank. (Actually it's a box with a notebook for a ledger. I told you he was careful with his money.) Caleb looks extremely sharp in the sunglasses and knows it. He thinks your package was an extra Christmas and has begun watching for more credit card applications in the mail.

More than the cool stuff, thank you for the wonderful way you have reminded me of the goodness of the people around us. I never expected a response to my letter. I assumed a faceless clerk would toss it in the trash. I too easily forget that there are real (and often good) people opening the mail I send and sending the mail I open. There are real (and often good) people standing in line at the bank and on the other end of the phone line. There are real (and often good) people in Wilmington, Delaware, whose realness and goodness I seldom appreciate.

I may not be as clever or generous as you have been, but I will try to do a better job of noticing people who expect to be ignored. I will try to more often act like a real and good person. Thank you.

Gratefully,

Brett Younger

If you get the chance, dance
July 2001

When PTA Queen Beth Miller asked if Carol and I would chaperone the sixth grade dance, Carol said, "Sure, it sounds like fun." It may surprise you, as it did us, to learn that our sixth grade son wasn't thrilled to hear that we were all going to the dance. Graham seemed to view the dance as the equivalent of a death sentence. The irony wasn't lost on me, a child who was forbidden to dance, now raising a child who refuses to do so. Graham only began to feel a little better when I agreed to introduce myself by saying, "Hi. I'm Gary Miller."

In the days before the dance I practiced lines I would never get to use in my deepest chaperone voice. "Put that out!" "Just what do you two think you're doing?" "Hey, what are you pouring in the punch bowl?" I decided the Puritan motto would be my own: "Someone somewhere is having a good time, and it must be stopped."

I also wanted to give my son some helpful pointers. I tried to think back to dances I went to when I was young, but of course, there were none. I, nonetheless, offered a couple of clever first lines: "So, do you come here often?" "Doesn't this song remind you of Frank Sinatra?" and my favorite, "See that cool guy over there. That's my dad."

When we arrived at Lake Air Middle School, we asked the parents in charge: "Should we be checking ID's or taking pictures or showing reluctant 11-year-olds how to bust a move?" We were told to sit quietly. Our only responsibility was to look old.

When we entered the wonderland that was the cafetorium, the fog machine was working its magic. Balloons floated to the ceiling, and the floor was covered with ribbons. The light show was vaguely reminiscent of the four-colored red, green, orange and blue spinning wheels that illuminated our Christmas trees in the 1960s.

The dance turned out to be five or six clumps of sixth graders, all male or all female clumps, standing around the edges of the dance floor. Every once in a while four or five children would hop in the middle as if they had pogo sticks while everyone else stared at them. Some of the not-yet-old-enough-for-acne boys played with the balloons, looking as out of place as Ralph Nader at an inauguration.

The disk jockey shouted into his microphone, "Lake Air, what's happening?" and "Scream if you don't like school." Whenever he said,

"Now we're going to slow it down," the crowd booed vociferously.

At one point, near the end, my son came over to where we were sitting quietly and cynically said, "Being a chaperone sure looks like hard work," to which I was kind enough to respond loudly, "I wish your father was here."

I've been reflecting on what I need to learn from my experience as a chaperone. Maybe it's something practical like "invest money in hearing clinics." Or perhaps I should learn something sociological like "My parents had a point" or "It's harder to be a kid nowadays" or "I'm really old."

While I was speculating on the meaning of it all, I heard a country song that they don't play at sixth grade dances. The last line is: "When you get the choice to sit it out or dance. I hope you dance."

If you have the chance to chaperone a dance, I hope you'll chaperone.

Celibate Celebration
October 2009

Alarm bells went off when the woman handed us two keys.

Carol and I recently celebrated 25 years of consistently joyful wedlock. As would be true for many interesting couples, we had different ideas on how to celebrate our anniversary. My plan was big and loud — a downtown hotel, a show, lobster dinner. Carol's plan was small and quiet — a retreat to the country, simple accommodations, simple meals. Carol frequently has the best ideas, hers was cheaper, and she made the reservations, so we spent our 25th anniversary at a monastery. Carol made it sound like fun — a romantic getaway, quiet conversation, walking hand-in-hand along the shore of the lake, tenderly reflecting on 25 years and lovingly dreaming the next 25.

Then the nun handed us two keys — as in two rooms, two rooms with single beds. Apparently the honeymoon cell had been booked. The quiet conversations were even quieter than we had imagined. Cistercian monks have taken a vow of silence. Talking is forbidden in the dining rooms, hallways and — this is the one that made us live in fear — guests' rooms. I should have learned more sign language.

We walked by the lake, but it was 95 degrees in August in Georgia and shorts are forbidden — a rule that even my Landmark Baptist grandmother would have thought harsher than a hair shirt. (The monk-y suits didn't look much more comfortable.)

The meals were simple, but not a good simple, not ham sandwich and potato chips simple. We had lots of "I would ask if these are sweet potatoes but I'm not allowed to talk" kind of simple.

At one point I snuck out to the GPS in the car and found a movie theater that was only six miles away, but I couldn't get Carol to give up her vows — and the front gate was locked each night at 8:00.

8:00 was when the "Grand Silence" began each night. Since we weren't allowed radios, cell phones, TV, musical instruments or speaking voices, I assumed this was the time at which we were no longer to bother others with the infuriating racket of turning pages.

8:00 may seem early, but it's not when vigils are at 4 a.m. What amazed me is that in the middle of the 4 a.m. worship service, there is a half hour of silence with the lights off, and no one fell asleep — at least I didn't see anyone sleeping, but my eyes weren't always open and the lights were off. Baptists should have a 4 a.m. service every now and then just to shame the people who complain that they can't get to Sunday school on time. We could have five worship services one day just to keep people from saying, "We're there every time the doors are open."

At midday prayers — one of the few times when speaking was allowed — the sister pointed us out and announced, "We have a couple here celebrating their 25th wedding anniversary." Everyone looked at us in befuddled silence. They wanted to mime, "What were you thinking?" I imagine that if monks decided to celebrate Easter in a Las Vegas casino, they might get similar looks.

But Carol was right. It ended up being a great place for a celebration. We chanted our gratitude and listened carefully for God's "You're welcome." We prayed, read, thought and wrote — only in part because there wasn't much else to do.

I have come to the conclusion that I admire monks the way I admire doctors. They do a much-needed work to which I am sure I am not called. Someone said that the prayers of the monastery hold the world together. Giving your life to prayer is an amazing countercultural commitment.

Monastic life isn't for all of us, but the disciplines of faith they follow are vital. The silence reminds us of the sacred importance of our words. The lack of conversation makes us long to share our lives. Bland food leads us to appreciate the occasional lobster dinner. Worship in the summer without air conditioning teaches us to focus. Singing our thanksgiving helps us to become people who know how to celebrate.

Caleb Younger on his father's preaching
July 2008

My 14-year-old son was asked to speak about my preaching at a Sunday school assembly. Here's what he said:

Preacher's kids listen to sermons differently. Normal kids listen with interest or take a much-deserved nap. I listen with fear — afraid that I'm about to be mentioned.

February 2001, my father's first sermon at Broadway Baptist Church
He preached: "I took a job in Indiana in 1986. Graham was born three years after that. We moved to Kansas in 1990. Caleb was born three years after that. We moved to Waco in 1996 and stopped forever our pattern of having a child three years after moving."

This seems innocuous, but it started a vicious pattern of mentioning me whenever he wants to sound clever.

April 2001
My dad preached: "Thank you to your ministers of housing Nancy and Jim in whose guest house I am staying. On Saturday night when my whole family was here, Caleb suggested that we could all move in to the Thurmonds' house."

I was only seven years old, but I don't think I seriously suggested that we live in someone else's house.

December 2003, the Sunday I was baptized and my 10th birthday
My dad preached: "Today my son turns the big one-o. After a decade you've seen a lot. You've skinned your knees on the sidewalk of life and said goodbye to your invisible friends. Caleb entertains his family with improvisational comedy that comes from somewhere other than our genes. He loves the agapé meal. His record is nine pitchers of tea. I was unimpressed with this number until the Thursday night I was given tea-pouring duty and fell seven pitchers short of the record. During the summer Caleb helps in the adult clothing room. He particularly likes calling out the name of the next person to be served. He thinks his specialty is pronouncing Hispanic names."

A few notes ... I still have my invisible friend. His name is José, and I'd rather not talk about him. The tea record is 11 pitchers. I don't do improvisational comedy. Like the great comedians, I prepare.

March 2004, after a spring break trip on which my father was pulled out of line at the airport for a security check
The next Sunday he preached: "The woman behind the counter said 'Uh, oh' — never a good sign. I'd like to think I was chosen at random, but it may have been my 'Peace on Earth' sweatshirt that made me a suspicious character. I was led down a long corridor with my family following behind me. Caleb was asking, 'What did Daddy do wrong?'"
I think he misheard me. What I actually said was, "They finally caught Daddy."

November 2004, my dad preached on my basketball tryouts
"On Saturday morning the air in the H.F. Stevens Middle School gym was thick with the smell of yesterday's heroes' sweat socks. The anxiety was palpable as they shot free throws. The line seemed 40 feet from the goal, but — and I probably shouldn't mention this — my son Caleb hit two of three."
The question is how much was my anxiety increased by the prospect of having my free throw percentage announced at church on Sunday morning.

August 2005, after our trip to Paris my dad talked about sitting next to a French family on the train

He preached: "An 11-year-old, Charlotte, offers me a potato chip. I say 'merci' — which exhausts my French. She says that she speaks 'a little English,' but she's actually quite good. When Caleb walks by, I introduce him to Charlotte."

It's bad enough to have your dad introducing you to French girls on a train, but how many people does he have to tell about it?

November 2005
Dad preached: "I find myself spending an increasingly large amount of time waiting for my children. I wait for Caleb's bus. I wait for Graham's basketball practice to end. I'm supposed to refrain from yelling 'Hey sweetie' when I first see them if their friends are around."

He never refrained.

February 2007
Dad preached: "On the Sunday after Christmas I was on vacation, so we visited another church. You know about mega-churches with praise teams, big screens and Starbucks in the lobby. This was the opposite. The processional began with bells and smells — a handbell ringer with no timing and a fog machine. Caleb was sitting nearest the aisle. When the cloud got to him we couldn't see him, but we heard him coughing."

I had a cold. Sue me. I had a cold. I could go on and on like my father does, but I've finally decided that he's doing it on purpose. He's figured out a way to make me listen. He wants me to listen because it might be about me. That's what good preachers do.

Life is short
October 2007

When our older son was born, friends came to the hospital, asked to hold the baby and commented on how glad they were that he looked like his mother. As they were leaving, several said something like, "Don't blink, because that's how long it will be before he's off to college."

They were right. In August we took our son to college. I find this hard to believe. It feels like he started crawling a month ago, went to kindergarten a week ago and got his driver's license a few days ago. It seems like only yesterday he was lying on the couch throwing food and making silly noises when actually it was two months ago.

The great American poet Dr. Seuss wrote:

How did it get so late so soon?
It's night before it's afternoon.
December is here before it's June.
My goodness how the time has flewn.
How did it get so late so soon?

It gets so late so soon. As the renowned philosopher Ferris Bueller said, "Life goes by pretty fast. If you don't stop and look around once in a while, you could miss it."

Life is too short for fantasy baseball, computer Solitaire or *Deal or No Deal*.

Life is too short for frozen pizza, bad novels or having the cleanest gutters on the block.

Life is too short to keep waiting for vacation, a special occasion or a better day.

Life is too short to sit around moping, choosing despair or worrying what people think.

Life is too short to be bitter over things you can't change, want to go back to what was or always do the same thing.

Life is too short to be bored, always blend in or sit in the corner while the band is playing.

Life is too short to intend a new life but never get around to it.

We shouldn't give ourselves to things that are less than God's best because life is short.

Life is short, so live every day as if it were your last, because some day you'll be right.

Life is short, so do what you love to do and give it your best.

Life is short, so recognize that today is the only day you have. Eat dessert first, and read good books.

Life is short, so go to church, stay awake and sing.

Life is short, so tell the truth, take care of this day and dance.

Life is short, so listen to the people you love, tell them how much they mean to you and visit someone else's mother in the nursing home.

Life is short, so recognize that every day is a special occasion. Look for excuses to laugh, and choose to be happy.

Life is short, so forgive. Look past the faults of others just like you hope they will do for you.

Life is short, so surround yourself with gracious people. Hug your friends and care for someone you haven't cared for before.

Life is short, so be courageous. Take a chance and live so that when your life flashes before your eyes, you'll have plenty to watch.

Life is short, so embrace the possibilities. Try something new. See that every day is an opportunity, and dream. But don't just dream; follow those dreams.

Life is short, so breathe and think deeply. Don't give your heart to that which won't fill your heart. And make the changes that will make the difference.

Life is short, so celebrate God's grace. Make time for the things that matter, and don't leave yourself regretting things you didn't do.

Pray hard. Believe in Christ with all of your soul, mind and strength because it's later than you think and life is short.

Why I am a patient driving instructor
February 2010

My son Caleb will be getting his driver's license in a couple of months. I have been an unexpectedly gracious coach: "That was only the curb, nothing to worry about." "I've always thought this garage was narrow." "For future reference, the brake is on the left."

There is a reason I am so patient. When I was 15 years old my father was the pastor of First Baptist Church, Saltillo, Miss. — the strictest church in the world. He preached loudly. Think John the Baptist with a better haircut. My father is a kind and caring man, but when I was growing up he frightened me.

At that time you could get a driver's license at 15. (That now seems about 10 years too soon.) My father insisted I drive the right way — hands at 10 and 2 o'clock, five miles below the speed limit, acting with utmost patience — "Don't ever drive in a hurry." As part of my teenage rebellion, when my dad wasn't in the car, I put my hands at 9 and 3 o'clock and went five miles above the speed limit.

One evening I got into a hurry driving home. I was the fourth car following a tractor down a two-lane road when I inexplicably decided to pass them all. I ended up rolling my father's car one and a half times and landing upside down in a ditch. As I began rolling I thought, "I am dead."

When the car stopped, I thought of my father. Once again, "I am dead."

I totaled my father's car. When the police officer asked who to call to come get me, I said, "Let me think about that." My mother wasn't home. My father was at the church, but I decided not to bother him right then. I would have the car towed to the garage. I could ride in the tow truck and then get a ride home. That would give me time to figure out how to tell him.

How could I have been so stupid? The inevitable grounding, the taking of the keys, and whatever corporal punishment he would come up with were all less terrifying than the fury he would undoubtedly unleash.

I was thinking about the judgment to come when I saw my father walking toward me. A helpful church member had seen me standing in the ditch by my father's overturned car and had called him. I decided to walk right up and tell him the whole truth so that he could immediately bundle me off to hell. I would use the prodigal son's speech: "Father, I have sinned against heaven and before you. I am no longer worthy to be called your son; treat me like one of your hired hands."

I started the speech, but I didn't get far. I was completely unprepared for what happened next. My father did the most painful, wondrous thing he could have done. I wouldn't have cried if he had done anything I had expected, but he took me in his arms and hugged me. All he said was, "I'm so glad you're okay."

On the ride home, the next day, and the next week I waited for him to get around to punishing me. I have been waiting for more than 30 years, but my dad has never reprimanded me for wrecking his car. Maybe he thought that forgiveness would be the best way to keep my hands at 10 and 2 o'clock and the accelerator at five miles below the speed limit. Maybe he didn't think about it at all. Maybe he was just glad I was okay.

The older I get, the more I think God's mercy works that way. God loves us, not out of strategic considerations, not because it will make us more of who we should be, though it may, but because that is who God is. God is always coming to embrace us, God's children.

Illustration by Scott Brooks

A preacher looks at 50
April 2011

Maybe the only thing I have in common with Bono, Amy Grant, Julianne Moore, Antonio Banderas, Cal Ripken, Julia Louis-Dreyfus, Wayne Gretzky, George Stephanopoulos and Fabio is that we all recently turned 50. I've been thinking about how to commemorate my Jubilee year. My friend Julie Pennington-Russell celebrated her 50th year by climbing Stone Mountain 50 times, so I'm considering eating 50 pizzas or watching 50 episodes of *MASH*.

Carol gave me an elliptical for my birthday — which I'm trying to figure out how to take as a compliment. I've heard that every minute you spend exercising adds another minute to your life. The problem is that you've spent that minute exercising.

Turning 50 wasn't really news to me. I've been getting older for some time. My mother stopped giving me a dollar per year 10 birthdays ago. I no longer order spicy food. I am afraid to drink Dr Pepper after 7 p.m. I eat less and weigh more. I haven't been to Luby's yet, but I hear the food is very good. Sometimes I nod my head when I have no idea what the person on the other side of the table just said. I'm this close to buying a magnifying glass. I take more time between haircuts. I have trouble remembering the capital of Vermont — it's Montpelier — even though I knew all of the capitals in the fourth grade. I am comfortable knowing that I will never again be awake for the end of the Oscars. It's almost certain that more of my life is behind me than ahead of me, but perhaps I'm only 50 years away from Willard Scott wishing me a happy birthday.

People seem confused about what to say. One 53-year-old offered this word of encouragement: "Turning 50 isn't the end of the world." One of my students exclaimed, "Happy quarter of a century!" — as though half a century was too antiquated to even imagine. Any minute now I will be replacing Wilford Brimley as the spokesperson for Quaker Oats.

I've been told about a dozen times that "50 is the new 30" — which makes no sense. I like to think that the writer of the country song with the line, "I'm old enough to know better, but still too young to care" is 50, but he's probably 30.

I understand the temptation to be the grumpy old man who complains that television shows don't tell stories, the music on the radio is noise and the Google machines are making us stupid, but the truth is I am happy to have an AARP card. I'm old enough to skip the cake and have my son bake a pie. My niece assures me that "The Bieber Decade" is going to be great.

Jimmy Buffett sings about "growing older but not up," but it is a good gift to recognize that you are growing older and up. I am not planning to be a late bloomer. I've figured out that some things are not going to happen, and I am fine with that. I'm not going to run a marathon or be on *Dancing with the Stars*.

Being 50 gives you perspective. When you're moving slower, you see more. Forgiveness comes easier. Prayer seems more natural. Most of my troubles are not nearly as big as I used to think.

My parents point out that 50 isn't 70, but it's not 30 either. Fifty is old enough to understand that life is too short not to live it like you will wish you had lived it when it is over. Fifty is an opportunity to give up on impressing anyone and enjoy the things you love while you can. Recognizing that we are on borrowed time helps us appreciate each day.

Fifty is a good time to ponder the rest of the path. There is still time for new beginnings, risks and dreams, but you also know to look for small wonders. I like being 50. I feel young again.

My mother, Ginger Rogers
May 2007

My mother should be a dancer. She would, of course, roll her eyes at this idea. All of her conservative Baptist life, dancing has been as off-limits as rock and roll, playing cards and Methodists. And yet, though she will deny it until Jesus comes back — which she would want me to point out could be any minute — my mother would be a magnificent dancer.

My mom has the athleticism of a ballet dancer. Her brief, but glorious, hoops career is legendary in Northeast Mississippi. Grandma wouldn't let my mother play basketball for the purple and gold of Itawamba High School because the team's short pants were two feet too short. On one famous night in 1948, several Lady Indians fouled out in the third quarter of a tight game with their bitter rivals — the Houston Hilltoppers — so the coach went into the stands to beg Clarice Graham to play. Mom slipped into a borrowed pair of boogie shoes and, in a dress that hit just below the ankles, scored several key baskets, dancing the Indians to a celebrated victory.

My mom has the precision of a ballroom dancer. Dancers have an extraordinary sense of where their feet, legs and arms should be at every second. Ginger couldn't spin with Fred if he showed up even one second late. My mother has a supernatural sense of where everyone should be and has never been less than 10 minutes early to anything. If punctuality were the key to dancing, my entire family would be June Taylor Dancers.

My mom has the spirit of a jitterbugger. The best dancers are passionate. Mom has the greatest laugh. When she giggles, which she frequently does, she begins to shake, her voice goes to a pitch audible only to dogs, her face turns a beautiful shade of red and her dark blue eyes start dancing. Her rhythmic exuberance would make Martha Graham, Cyd Charisse and Paula Abdul jealous.

When I was home for the summer during college, I often irritated my mother by trying to get her to dance with me. On a few occasions she humored me with a couple of steps, but she would never admit her true interest in the kicker steps I had learned from the dancing bears at Baylor. I pointed out that King David danced, the psalmists tell us to praise God with dance, and Ecclesiastes assures us that there is a time to dance, but she still wouldn't waltz, tango or foxtrot with her son.

Angela Monet writes, "Those who danced were thought to be quite insane by those who could not hear the music." I feel certain that though she still hasn't admitted it, mom hears the music and knows she should be dancing.

Some can only remember the jigs their now-departed mothers danced. Some mothers are too far away to two-step with their sons. Only a fortunate few can put their arms around their mothers and dance.

On Mother's Day, be thankful for every playful step your mother ever took. Any excuse is good enough to trip the light fantastic with our moms, even if it's only in our imaginations.

The birds and bees (and how they fly)
June 2007

I was 10 years old, lying on my bed on a Saturday afternoon reading an Archies comic book. (I'm only a little embarrassed to admit that I liked Veronica more than Betty.) My father came in wearing his sober Ward Cleaver face. "Brett, put your novel away. There's something I should have talked to you about by now, but I've been putting it off, because I wasn't sure you were old enough to understand. We're going to have a serious conversation that I hope you'll remember. I want you to listen carefully. Let's go to the den to talk."

As I followed him out of my room, I was thinking exactly what you're thinking. My father had just offered Robert Young's introduction to the birds-and-the-bees talk. What I wanted to say, however, was, "Dad, you gave this speech a month ago. It was disconcerting. I'm not sure I want to hear it again. You said that if I had any questions I should check back. I will never do that, but I appreciate the offer."

How could my father forget that we'd already had this discussion? ("Discussion" in this context means he talked and I listened.) And yet, inexplicably, he had forgotten. It was going to be at least five tortuous minutes before I learned who Archie was taking to the big dance at Riverdale High.

I fully expected to hear, "Brett, when a man and a woman love each other very much …" but instead Dad opened with, "Brett, it's time to talk about how an airplane flies." Only then did I notice that several model airplanes — visual aids — were waiting for us in the den.

My father gave a speech that lasted a lot longer than the expected five minutes: "An airplane flies because its wings create lift, the upward force on the plan, as they interact with the flow of air around them. The wings alter the direction of the flow of air as it passes."

About when I thought he would be getting to, "a woman is different from a man …" he was saying: "The exact shape of the surface of a wing is critical to its ability to generate lift. The speed of the airflow and the angle at which the wing meets the oncoming air stream contribute to the amount of lift generated."

We didn't get to first dates or anything remotely interesting, but Dad completely covered drag, acceleration and aeronautical theory.

Thirty-six years later I more often recall Dad's "how planes fly" sermon than his "where babies come from" speech. I appreciate the "everything you always wanted to know about aviation" address, because it was my father at his best.

He worked hard to pass down his love for model airplanes (we both tried, but I never got it), the Dallas Cowboys (my teenage rebellion was rooting against America's Team), westerns (I like *The Searchers*), Frank Sinatra (it took a while, but I'm right with him now), and Mexican food (we completely agree that enchiladas are nature's perfect food).

Good fathers share what they love. Father's Day is a reminder to be thankful for every gift our fathers tried to give us — even the flying lessons that never got off the ground.

Runaway bunnies
April 2012

The graduates sang a rousing rendition of "We're on Our Way to Kindergarten." Mrs. Ayres gave out the "Certificates of Completion." (They went in alphabetical order. Youngers learn to be patient.) We had cupcakes and cookies and then stepped out into the bright light of the post pre-kindergarten world.

I enjoyed graduation, but the real rite of passage took place earlier that morning in my office at 8:05. Almost three years earlier, Caleb began attending the Children's Center at our church two mornings a week. On his first day Caleb was apprehensive, so we took three books from home (*Spot Counts from 1 to 10*, *But Not the Hippopotamus*, and *The Runaway Bunny*) to read before going downstairs. The next day we read the same three books. We kept them on my shelf, but soon decided to pick a book from the church library each day. We quickly had a full-blown ritual. We would drop Graham off at school, park in front, unlock the door, turn on the lights, go to the library, pick out a book, and read it in my office.

As a 4-year-old, Caleb came to the Children's Center three mornings a week. The next year, it was five mornings. So, we read in my office more than 300 mornings. We learned about nature (*Our Yard Is Full of Birds*). We read books with noises (*The Very Quiet Cricket*) and blinking

lights (*The Very Lonely Firefly*). We made friends with *Corduroy, Babar, Chrysanthemum,* and *Wilfrid Gordon McDonald Partridge.* We introduced discussions on the family with *Daddy Makes the Best Spaghetti* — my favorite — and dealt with social issues such as prejudice (*Frog and Toad Together*) and war and peace (*The Butter Battle Book*). We tackled theology with *God Made It All, Carol Beth Learns about Following Jesus* and *When I Talk to God.*

As we opened the front door on our last day of pre-kindergarten, I said: "Caleb, this is the last morning we'll read a book before going downstairs, so pick a good one." He thought about it for a long time. I thought he would choose a recent favorite — *The Little Baby Snoogle Fleejer, The Cowboy and the Black-eyed Pea,* or *the Giant Jam Sandwich.* Instead my suddenly very grown-up soon-to-be-kindergartner said, "Let's read the old ones."

It may have been the last time that I heard *Spot Counts from 1 to 10.* We counted one cow chewing, two horses trotting and three ducks swimming. We squealed with four piglets squealing, clucked at five chickens clucking, and when 10 bees buzzed we shut the book fast before any could escape.

We read *But Not the Hippopotamus* in unison. We reminisced with the hog and the frog cavorting in the bog, the cat and two rats trying on hats, the moose and the goose who together have juice, and the bear and the hare who went to the fair. When the animal pack came running on back saying "Hey come join the lot of us" and "She just didn't know. Should she stay? Should she go?" … we shouted joyfully "But yes the hippopotamus!" and feigned tears on "But not the armadillo."

The Runaway Bunny, not normally a tearjerker, got to me. The little bunny (just like, I imagine, every pre-kindergarten graduate) feels a need to put some distance between him and his parents. His mother keeps saying, "If you run away, I will run after you. You are my little bunny." If he becomes a fish, she will be a fisherman. If he becomes a rock on the mountain, she will be a mountain climber. If he becomes a bird, she will be a tree to which he comes home. By the time we read that if he became a little boy she would be his mother and catch him in her arms and hug him, I was telling Caleb that my allergies were acting up.

My little bunny is now waiting on college admission letters. Caleb will graduate from high school next month. This graduation may feel even more momentous than pre-kindergarten. In our mushiest moments we know that the love we know overwhelms all the sorrow we feel.

Ballpark Fare

Someone left the lights on, and I'm just trying to jog past them
February 2000

Every once in a great while I see a jogger and react in a way that is incomprehensible to thinking people: I say to myself, "I should start jogging." (I recognize that many intelligent people feel that the more understandable response to runners is to turn the steering wheel ever so slightly so that they run back up on the curb where they belong.)

My unexplainable longing to jog usually doesn't last long enough for me to put on my tennis shoes, but on rare occasions I forget how much I hate jogging and run (throughout this column, I will be using the verb "run" in the broad, general sense) for a few days.

The key to my success as a runner (I am using the noun "runner" in the same general sense) is that I don't run very far (I am not embarrassed by embarrassingly short distances) or very fast (it can take several minutes for me to pass a parked car). The only part of jogging at which I excel is "jogger's face." While runners claim that they enjoy running, the look on most joggers' faces is complete anguish. Even though I don't jog far enough or fast enough to qualify for any genuine anguish, whenever a car or another jogger passes I huff and puff and contort my face as if my heart, lungs and every muscle in my body are about to explode. When they are out of sight, I sit on the curb and rest.

For a couple of weeks I ran around a couple of blocks near our house. The whole trip was less than a mile (I say this only to prove that I was telling the truth when I said that I am not embarrassed by embarrassingly short distances). The highlight of my jaunt was an out-of-the-ordinary yard about 4/10 of a mile from our house. At night, when the lights are on, you can spot it from about 3/10 of a mile away. The most striking feature is the Christmas lights. The lights, which are in a Mulberry tree, are a startling variety of colors. There's also a red birdhouse with a black roof and an invitation to "See Rock City." A big red bow adorns a holly wreath. Orange, purple, pink, red and white gladiolas and lilies cover every spare inch. I hope I never have to use my jogger's face near this spot, because it's hard not to smile at this yard.

Not long after I started jogging I had a conversation with some people who lived in the area. I asked, "What's the story with your neighbor's Christmas lights? That's an interesting yard." They quickly made it clear that the yard is not as amusing to them as it is to me: "Those stupid Christmas lights have been up for years ... It makes me furious when I think about what that yard does to my property values ... I am sorely tempted to buy a BB gun just to shoot those lights ... &%$*!@."

I started to rethink my feelings. Perhaps the yard wasn't as wonderful as I originally thought. Maybe I would feel differently if I lived nearby. Perhaps 4/10 of a mile into my run, I was experiencing the "jogger's euphoria" about which veteran joggers talk.

One Sunday evening I was gradually, leisurely making my way around the neighborhood when I saw a woman working in "the yard" just up ahead. I sped up so that 10 minutes later, when I was in need of a break anyway, I was able to stop and say: "Your yard is really interesting. Is there a story behind the Christmas lights?"

She smiled and said, "Yes, there is." She pointed to the house across the street and identified a particular window. "The elderly woman who lives there came to stay with her children seven years ago. She's in her 90s now and seldom leaves her room. After her first Christmas here she went on and on about how much she enjoyed looking at the lights and bright colors in our yard. We're the only view she has. When Christmas was over, we didn't have the heart to take the lights down. We decided that as long as she's around, we'll leave the lights on."

How many times are our aggravations someone else's Christmas lights?

Leave the lights on.

In the big inning, God created baseball

September 2003

This is the time of year when our minds turn to one of the neglected spiritual disciplines. We recognize prayer, scripture reading and meditation throughout the year, but in September our attention turns especially to baseball.

The spiritual aspects of baseball are undeniable. The goal is to be "safe" (saved) until you can go "home" (God's eternal presence).

Watching a baseball game is following the psalmist's admonition to "Be still." In a world that's too busy, baseball is countercultural — sit, relax, reflect. The mystic Yogi Berra pointed out baseball's contemplative qualities: "Ninety percent of the game is half mental."

Unlike other sports, baseball is timeless. No clock counts down the seconds. People who complain that baseball is slow miss the point — dreams are slow; hope is slow; spirituality is slow. The great Yogi puts it, "It ain't over till it's over." Some of the elements of the game change (try not to think about the abominations of artificial turf and designated hitters), but baseball itself is eternal.

Baseball is time set aside to pay attention, so look at the angle of the bat, the ball no bigger than an aspirin traveling as fast as a bullet, and the ballet of the fielders diving. Watch all the back-bending, knee-stretching and torso-revolving that go on in the on-deck circle.

See how stepping into the batter's box is a ritual unto itself for slow-moving players. Watch how frequently and forcefully ballplayers spit and how involved they are with dirt — rubbing dirt into their gloves, tossing dirt to test the wind, and tapping dirt off their spikes with their bat. "You can observe a lot by watching," Berra once said.

Join the choir singing "The Star Spangled Banner" and "Take Me Out to the Ballgame." Hope for stolen bases, double plays and more knuckleball pitchers, but lean forward only on 3-2 counts.

This sport, above all others, is about penitence. "We made too many wrong mistakes" (Yogi). Believe the promise of Numbers 15:28, "The priest shall make atonement before the Lord for the one who commits an error."

Bartlett Giamatti wrote: "Baseball breaks your heart. It is designed to break your heart. The game begins in the spring, when everything else begins again, and it blossoms in the summer, filling the afternoons and evenings, and then as soon as the chill rains come, it stops, and leaves you to face the fall alone."

God speaks to different people through different disciplines. Long ago I passed the point where the "old" players are younger than I am, but baseball continues to make me feel alive. It's a sign of hope for me that when life is loud and rushed, there is still baseball. I suppose it's possible to feel the cool breeze of the Spirit at a basketball game or imagine Jesus at a football game, but neither seems likely to me.

Jacques Barzun wrote, "Whoever wants to know the heart and mind of America had better learn baseball." Would it be too much too say, "Whoever wants to know the heart and mind of God had better learn baseball"?

Yes, of course it would, but take your soul to a ballgame and give thanks to the God of Abraham, Isaac and Jacob; Willie, Mickey and the Duke; the God of bread and wine, peanuts and Cracker Jacks; the God of grace and glory, shoestring catches and curve balls; the God of the baptistery and the pitcher's mound; the God of new wineskins and old baseball fans.

Like no one's watching
May 2005

All-star second baseman Alfonso Soriano and I were on television together — sort of. On Staff Appreciation Day — which ought to rank just behind Easter and Christmas among church holidays — my family hit the jackpot. We received tickets to a Texas Rangers' game.

When I buy tickets we sit close to teenage fans with painted faces, pigeons and God. Since "bleachers" and "upper bleachers" are about the same, I don't pay much attention to where our seats are located. But on this occasion I noticed "VIP infield, Row 1." I thought our friend was kidding when she handed me the tickets and said, "Dress well, because you're right behind the plate. You'll be on TV the whole time."

When we got to the game I decided we were far enough toward first base that we weren't on TV. Not being televised made it easier to sit back, relax and enjoy watching millionaires scratch themselves.

Then during the third inning Carol's parents called to tell us that of the 44,348 at the ballpark, the four of us were the ones in living color. We had been warned, "If you're on TV, don't be the guy who talks on his cell phone and waves, 'Look, Ma, I'm on TV'" so we tried to stay calm.

Illustration by Scott Brooks

My father-in-law wanted to know why we were unhappy. None of us thought we were unhappy, but now we felt the need to look giddy. We could wave our arms and cheer, but the camera was on us only until the batter made contact.

Gesticulating wildly when nothing was going on would have been peculiar. Carol decided to say "hello" to her mom in sign language. The sign for "Grandma" is not subtle — a thumb to the chin and 10 fingers extended like a spider. Those who do not know sign language could interpret it as an obscene gesture. I began to think I should have dressed differently. I was wearing a plain blue T-shirt, which seemed reasonable, but now I wondered if I should have worn a T-shirt that makes a statement — "Amnesty International," "Bread for the World" "*Baptists Today*" ... Maybe I should have dyed my hair and held up "John 3:16." Could I have gotten people to look up "Isaiah 22:18"? "God will seize firm hold of you, whirl you round and round and throw you like a ball."

In the sixth inning we discovered that Graham, our 15-year-old, had eaten two thirds of our peanuts before we left home. This would normally lead to a gentle reprimand, but no one wants to lecture their child on Channel 27.

Caleb, our 11-year-old, decided to go for cotton candy. I thought it would make me look like a good father, so I went with him. Should we buy pink or blue? Which looks better?

We watched a tape the day after the game. The Toronto Blue Jays, who lost 11-2, looked better than we did. Why didn't we tell Graham to put his feet down? Why didn't we kiss when the Rangers scored? Why does eating a sucker make you look like one? Why did I take off my cap? So here's what I learned from my brush with stardom. The camera really does add 10 pounds. Sunglasses make even the gentlest minister look like a member of the Mafia. And most obviously, caring that somebody is watching keeps you from enjoying yourself.

Reinhold Niebuhr said that we need a "genuine Christian nonchalance" — indifference to the foolishness in the world. He means that Christians shouldn't care about the stupid things other people care about. But next time I will get a haircut.

Hoop dreams (or nightmares)
September 2004

Two weeks before youth camp, Graham casually said: "I'm going to enter the camp three-on-three basketball tournament. John, Robert and I are playing, but we can have a fourth person in case one of us breaks a leg. Do you want to be on the team?"

I was so delighted that joy overwhelmed good sense. "Son, I would love to be on your team." A week later when Robert learned he couldn't go to camp, I didn't fully recognize the implications.

The other teams had cool names like Los Pollos Locos, Flying Jungle Hippos and Charlie's Angels. I wanted to be Loser's Bracket, but The Brotherhood has a Baptist ring to it.

My best game was our first round bye — I had no missed shots, turnovers or broken bones.

Before our game against Fellowship of Believers from Hereford, the referee — who wasn't in the gym during the games — explained the rules: "Games are to 11, twos count one, threes count two." I asked, "How many time-outs do we get?" but he ignored me.

I was pleased to discover that not only is my son good, but so is John. Since John was a counselor I assumed he was slow, but he is 17 years younger than I am. If we were the Beatles, John and Graham would be John and Paul and I would be Ringo. I would not be carrying the scoring load. I made one basket in our initial game — a scoring average I maintained throughout the tournament. I quickly learned that the gym contained little oxygen and that the line between warming up and tiring out is now non-existent. We won when my son made a long two-pointer. On Wednesday morning my legs were a little sore. I conserved energy by taking the elevator instead of the stairs and lying down in the shower.

We next played ROWF (didn't ask what it stood for) from Highland Park Baptist in Austin. This team kept making substitutions, bringing in fresh legs. I called out "Robert" several times, but as he was in Fort Worth taking an SAT preparation class, he did not respond. My favorite play — and I'm still paying for this — was diving, well, falling really, on a loose ball and wrestling a terrified teenager. We won on a long two-pointer by my son. When it was over, the terrified one politely said, "Good game, Grandpa."

Our third game was with A Few Nice Gentlemen from First Baptist, Austin. They had the best uniforms — purple socks and tuxedo T-shirts with cool names like 3s Please, El Niño and J-time. Graham had written "The Brotherhood" on a white T-shirt with the sleeves ripped off, but any intimidation this created was lost when a girl from our youth group outlined it with a pink marker. So as not to run out of clothes, I wore the same shirt each game. By the last game my shirt kept opponents from guarding me closely (or they saw no need to guard me closely). The game ended when my son hit a long two-pointer.

On Thursday morning I could not move my legs or arms. The championship game was against the aforementioned ROWF, determined to avenge their earlier embarrassment against a team described during the awards ceremony as "two old guys and a freshman." One of our youth offered to keep stats on how many points I scored. I suggested he count how many players I ran into. (He says it was seven, but that seems low.) We won on a long two-pointer by my son.

Ministers have different goals for youth camp at different times in their lives. "Survival," for instance, has been steadily moving up my list. I'm no longer expecting epiphanies. This year my son and I won a basketball tournament for the first and last time, and I was so glad to be his father. I'm taking it as one of my favorite moments of the grace of God.

A warm spot for benchwarmers
January 2012

Sitting on the bench has a lousy reputation, but it's undeserved. Motivational speakers encourage us to "Get off the bench! Get into the game!" How do they not understand that if we're on the bench it's not by choice? Our decision is whether to sit on the bench or quit the team. Who decided that picking on the people on the bench is fair?

My son is a senior on the varsity basketball team at Parkview High School. Making the team with my genes is no small accomplishment. Parkview has 2,700 students. Caleb is 5'7" and a reasonable speed in a sport that rewards tall and fast. He's pretty good. Last year on the junior varsity he started several games. Whenever he made a great play I felt like I was cheering for someone else's child. He's a smart player who hustles, but it's finally caught up with him that he can't dunk. His game takes place several feet below the rim.

We're now parents who bring a book. When our team wins or loses by 20 points we happily watch our son play the last three minutes, but when I look at Caleb on the bench I couldn't be more proud. He claims he's there to hold up the team GPA, but he knows how to sit on the bench. He listens during time-outs. He fist-bumps players coming back to the bench. He is appropriately despondent when his team loses. "That's my boy" means more this year. My son has never seemed more like a chip off the old block.

I spent some of the best hours of my life on the bench. My first bench was in Little League baseball. I sat next to Coach Harbour who was like a gracious uncle taking care of his myopic nephew. I was on the bench, in part, because I couldn't judge a fly ball. Anything 10 feet off the ground was an adventure. I was a blind squirrel trying to catch a nut with a glove.

Baseball benches are good because they're in a dugout, which is like a really cool clubhouse, except we were allowed to spit on the floor. Most of us spit sunflower seeds, but a few of the 12-year-olds chewed tobacco (it was Mississippi). Bench warmers had important responsibilities like arranging the bats in order by size. We were the ones who shouted at the opposing team's hitters, "Hey batter batter." The bench was a great place from which to enjoy a game.

I would have sat on the bench during junior high football if Coach

Buse had allowed benches. He felt strongly that players who weren't in the game should stand. I didn't like football, but every male without a doctor's excuse was expected to be on the team (it was Mississippi). I enjoyed the pep rallies and the bus ride to the games. My one attempt at dipping snuff was on the football bus. It was particularly good that I didn't play that night.

I was a second-string wide receiver on a team that had no pass plays. I prayed for the first-string wide receiver to stay healthy. The other team invariably included large, violent young men who enjoyed hitting smaller people. Coach Buse seemed angry that I weighed 120 pounds. He made Bear Bryant look soft.

My last bench was in the gym. For most, basketball was a way to kill time between football and spring football (it was Mississippi), but I love basketball. I was better at hoops, but by my last year I had a place on the bench with my short, slow friends. Coach Coggins was encouraging, "That was a fine idea, Brett. If you were Pistol Pete Maravich, you might have pulled it off." He forgave me for being 5'7".

Caleb is an excellent bench warmer. We enjoyed it when my son got to play every game, but it's easy to be happy when you're getting to play. Sitting on the bench is the real test of character. Some who could be sitting on the bench decided it was too hard and quit. Caleb could have chosen to make it to all the meetings of the Latin Club.

God doesn't just love the tall and fast. God understands that most of us spend a significant amount of time on the bench. Some of the best Christians in the sanctuary never sit on the platform. Some of the most dedicated choir members never get to sing a solo. Some of the most loving followers of Jesus aren't on the cover of *Baptists Today*. Some of God's favorite players sit on the bench.

Service with a smile
February 2012

Parents of varsity basketball players are not asked if they would like to work the concession stand; we are handed a schedule. Couples deciding whether to have children should consider how they feel about hawking hot dogs.

I show up early for my shifts, so I will have time to familiarize myself with that day's specials. I pick up pointers from Mavis and Bob. Imagine Paula Deen and Gordon Ramsay in the same kitchen. I learn how to talk like a real waiter.

"Can I help you even though you're wearing an Alabama shirt?"

"Will that be dine in or carry out?"

"How do you want your popcorn cooked?"

"The red skittles make you dizzy, the yellow ones make your hair curly, and the blue ones make you look like you've been kissing a Smurf."

"You understand that two orders of chili cheese fries is not a meal."

"We need another shrimp étouffée!"

"How about some hot sauce with that pickle?"

"The hamburgers are a tender cut of corn-fed Midwestern beef, USDA prime at its best. It's the rich flavor of sirloin coupled with the tenderness of a filet. You can have it with mustard or ketchup, but if you want both you have to buy another burger."

"Enjoy that Coke while you can. When you're my age you'll be ordering diet everything. Plus you know it's rotting your stomach lining."

"I think it's great that you drink pink PowerAde. Lots of guys would think it's feminine."

"We also have clear PowerAde, but we put it in water bottles."

"It's two cookies for a dollar, four cookies for two dollars, or everything on the counter for a hundred dollars."

"This dollar bill looks counterfeit."

Know your clientele. Ten-year-olds seem to enjoy witty repartee more than 15-year-olds who tend to roll their eyes.

People stare at the menu over our heads as though they are trying to figure out a complicated physics equation. We get some goofy questions: "Do you take credit cards?" "Could I have some lemon for my water?" "What's healthy?"

We have repeat customers who think of the concession stand as a five-course meal — Cheetos for the appetizers, green skittles for the salad course, cheese nachos for the soup, pizza for the main course (hot and ready after just 25 seconds in the microwave), and Otis Spunkmeyer's finest for dessert.

I advise customers to get to the concession stand early in the game. (None of the food is getting any better.) If you're worried about germs, order things in wrappers (like Snickers bars) or eat at home.

I've learned that when a 7-year-old gives you five quarters for a $1.50 hot dog, you hand it to them and say, "Don't let your dog bite you."

Unlike some of the wait staff, I like being 50 feet from the pep band — whose favorite song is the classic "Louie, Louie." Everything is more fun when you have to shout.

I have considered putting out a tip jar. If I label it "Bribes for the Refs," we might do pretty well.

On one recent shift I realized that our customers were self-selecting. The teenage girls were going to the handsome player from my son's team. The teenage boys were going to the varsity girls' team's star. Everyone over 40 was coming to me. I pointed this out to my two young co-workers and got a look that embodied the word, "Duh."

I have discovered that I like saying, "Do you want some fries with that?" I find great joy in being the one who knows where the extra napkins are. My hour-and-a-half shifts fly by.

Most people don't want a future in the fast food industry. It is hard work when it is eight hours a day, five days a week. On career day the line at the "Service Industry" booth is short. "Community Service" is a form of punishment.

And yet, "How can I help you?" is a Christ-like question. Jesus suggested that we try "to serve and not to be served." Perhaps Jesus suggested we serve others, in part, because it can be fun.

The audacity of hoops
March 2009

On March 16 — the day after Selection Sunday — four NCAA college basketball tournament brackets will be on our refrigerator. Every year my family enjoys picking the games and seeing which one of us picks the most winners.

Actually, that's not completely true. The one who wins will enjoy it and the rest will not. (We do this for entertainment purposes only; no wagering is allowed.) I look forward to staring at my bracket, trying to convince myself that I know something about St. Mary's basketball. I'm already relatively certain how this dance will turn out.

Carol will use an amazing system that has served her well. She will pick Missouri because her parents used to live there, Butler because she has relatives named Butler, and IUPUI because it's fun to say. If some pesky team like Alabama State beats some big dog like Connecticut, Carol will have picked it because everyone knows hornets would give huskies fits. If this year is like most, her whimsical Nostradamus-like prognostication will put Carol well ahead of *Sports Illustrated*'s so-called experts.

In his early years in the tournament, my younger son was bitten by picking too many UNC-Ashevilles, Vermonts, and Holy but not that athletic Crosses, so for the last few years Caleb has been the champion of the champions. He will cast his lot with the Dukes, North Carolinas and Pittsburghs — the giants of the basketball world. Caleb has no room for high hoops hopes, only the solid hardwood of the expected. If there are no upsets, Caleb will have his bracket laminated.

I am somewhere in the middle. I will end up regretting picking Mississippi State. I have to learn that it's wrong to pick a team just because my mother gave me their cap. I will be right to pick Wake Forest because Demon Deacons is the all-time greatest nickname. I will be wrong to go against Oklahoma because their players don't go to class. I will wish I hadn't picked Marquette just because Marquette was my favorite Jesuit missionary.

If this year is like most, I will once again grow in my admiration of our older son. Graham will end up with a broken, bleeding bracket, but in the truest sense he will far outdistance us all. Graham chooses not to be part of the world where UCLA, Syracuse and Louisville win games, but lose their souls.

For years Graham's bracket included predictions of Western Kentucky taking out Kentucky, Texas A&M-Corpus Christi knocking off Texas, and George Mason eliminating Georgetown. Graham picked upsets that could only happen in his hoop dreams. He continually gave his heart to directional schools (Northern Iowa, North Dakota State, South Alabama), initialed schools (VMI, VCU, BYU), and states that don't sound like states (Weber State, Portland State, Long Beach State). His love for the Gonzagas, Buffalos and Mercers kept him from winning, but it also kept him in love with the audacity of hoops.

A year ago Graham became a freshman at Davidson College. This was perfect, because Graham prefers the world where the Davidson Wildcats could win it all — and last year they came close. Davidson snuck into the tournament as a #10 seed. They beat a #7, a #2, a #3 and then lost to #1 Kansas, the eventual champion, on a last-second shot. They won almost as many games as my hope-filled son predicted.

Graham does not live in the black and white of boring brackets, but in the rainbows of which dreams are made. He has chosen a world in which small, liberal arts colleges with no athletic tradition and no rebounding could take the trophy. It is, of course, madness, but if dreams are madness, then we should choose not the NCAA tournament of what will be, but the hope of what should be.

People of faith regularly put faith in the Davidsons of the world. We keep believing that David will defeat Goliath. The Christian gospel is the good news of the unexpected. We don't give ourselves to what is most likely. We give ourselves to what is best. We dream of a world that is better than it is.

Telling the truth
November 2005

Two of my favorite choir members graciously invited our family to sit with them in a luxury suite at a Dallas Cowboys' football game. It seemed like fun. My children love sports. Carol loves a party. They promised there would be food. None of us had ever been to Texas Stadium. It's a generous invitation. The parking pass cost more than my first suit. So I said, "We'd love to go."

But secretly I had reservations. It's a complicated story. When I was growing up, my father was the biggest Cowboys fan in the world. Tom Landry was only a notch below Billy Graham. My mother once said that my father loved Roger Staubach more than he loved her. His response was that he loved her more than Calvin Hill. We moved breakable furniture out of the living room before Dallas games, but still lost a couple of lamps. My father was exuberant in expressing his devotion.

All teenagers find some way to rebel against their parents. Some do drugs, drink or sleep around. I didn't do any of those things, but what I did may have been more painful to my father.

When I was 14 — and I'm not proud of this — I started cheering against Dallas. Whenever a Cowboy got arrested — and it was rather frequent in the 1970s — I cut the story out of the newspaper and helpfully taped it to the refrigerator. On one occasion during grace before a meal I prayed for wide receiver Bob Hayes' cocaine problem. I was sent to my room without dinner. I've been pulling for whoever is playing Dallas for a long time. My children have now inherited this unattractive part of who I am. Of course, I recognize that many fine and wonderful people pull for the Cowboys, and there are moments, especially since I moved to Fort Worth, when I wish I could be 13 again and be one of them, but those days are long gone.

So on the way to Texas Stadium we practiced our non-partisan cheers: "That was some play."

"That guy is big."

"Those cheerleaders must work out a lot."

"Bill Parcells could work out a little more, couldn't he?"

Luckily, most of the focus in our suite was on the food — shrimp, ribs, chicken, hamburgers. There may have been some vegetables, but I'm not sure. The caramel chocolate cake was the highlight of the second half.

I used my non-partisan cheers:
"Let's go team."
"We want a touchdown."
"Run fast."

I slipped once and shouted, "That was a terrible call" at a referee who had made a call that the 54,000 people seated around me thought was wonderful. I tried to save myself with, "but the angle is such that I couldn't really see it from here."

One of our church's fifth grade Sunday school teachers cheered the loudest of anyone in our suite. I kept my distance as he repeatedly yelled, "Kill 'em."

We had a lovely time, but it was tempered a little by the feeling that I wasn't quite telling the truth. I have friends with whom I don't mention certain subjects, and that keeps us from being better friends. I know that some issues will always divide us and arguing doesn't do much good, but not telling the truth begins to feel like a lie. Rather than dishonest silence we need to follow St. Paul's advice, "Speak the truth in love."

This is hard to do, and we have difficulty with it. Sometimes we avoid speaking truth in fear of offending someone, and sometimes we speak the truth so coarsely that we don't display love at all, but cold, hard arrogance instead. The best friends learn to share who they are without putting down those who disagree. The best churches learn to be honest without being judgmental.

Sometimes we need to say, "You need to know how hard it is for me to hear racist comments" or "I've never told you how much I appreciate you" or "If I'm going to be your friend, I need to tell you how important my Christian faith is to me" or "I'm sorry I root against the Cowboys."

The young and the waistless, the old and the beautiful
January 2010

On most Saturday mornings I go to Mountain Park Park *(Note to the editor — that's not a typo. It really is the name of the park. Mountain Park is the name of the city). (Second note to the editor — maybe you should leave the previous note in the column. It might be funny.) (Third note — do you think you should leave in the second note, too?)*

My park is set up for old people and small children. The track winds around tennis courts where everyone plays doubles, a playground with tiny slides and swings, and a pond with old ducks. The mile-long path has wooden markers each tenth of a mile, offering encouragement to runners every couple of minutes.

"Run" may not be exactly the right word to describe what usually goes on at my park. "Jog" would be closer. "Trot," "lope" and "saunter" fit. We go slow. We time our miles by the position of the sun.

My crowd wears knee braces, warm-up pants and "Carter/Mondale" T-shirts. We include lots of moms with strollers. (I have only seen one mother smoking while out getting her baby some fresh air.)

Our children have given us iPods so we don't talk much, but we recognize one another and (even as we listen to Tony Bennett) nod in a friendly manner. We admire one another, because we know it takes more than a New Year's resolution to keep people like us showing up.

I've named one of the regulars "Rocky." He wears an orange University of Tennessee visor. He must be in his 80s. The way he runs

Illustration by Scott Brooks

makes me think at least one hip and one knee are recent additions. He moves slowly, but he is often at it when I arrive and still at it when I leave.

"Mabel" waited too long to start substituting the side salad for the fries. I'm guessing she is there on doctor's orders. It is easy to imagine her a few years after her kids left home suddenly surprised that she is wearing XXL. She brings a white poodle — "Killer" — who keeps her moving, though not always in the right direction.

When I got to the park one recent Saturday, I immediately knew something was terribly wrong. Young people in $200 Nikes were dashing around at a startling pace. The high school cross-country team had invaded our family-friendly track. A thundering herd of 16-year-olds with 2 percent body fat (even though they still eat double cheeseburgers) were running five-minute miles like they owned the place. They were frightening our ducks.

What had always been a leisurely stroll now felt like running with the bulls of Pamplona. Parents cheered their sons wildly. Coaches lined the way with stop watches and megaphones. If the enthusiastic crowd even noticed slow-moving people like Mabel and me, it must have been with condescension.

At first I felt bitter about being run off the road, but after the whippersnappers left I calmed down and began to wonder whether the wrong people are getting the applause.

Who are the real runners? It takes more for my gang to be there than the 100-pounders with teenage knees. Mabel sweats, labors and struggles, but she keeps coming. Most people Rocky's age have given up, but he still shows up. Maybe the 10th graders darting around the track will still be at it 40 years from now, but isn't the applause premature?

The runners we should admire the most may not be the young fast ones, but the grandparents who drag themselves out of bed when they are feeling sore all over.

The real heroes and heroines may not get the loudest ovations. The quickest, smartest and best looking should not get all of the praise. The best Sunday school teacher may not be the one with the biggest class, but the gracious friend who has been caring for the same good people for decades. The best pastor may not be the one with the biggest church, but the minister who faithfully serves a congregation that struggles to survive. God's finest are the ones — young and old, large and small — who are not running for applause.

Regional Specials

Your guide to the Holy Land
September 2010

After two weeks in Israel, I feel qualified to offer the kind of advice you might expect only from tour guides with years of experience.

Try to get to the Holy Land as a young person. If you are as old as 49, you may find the mountains exhausting and the heat draining. Fill your pockets with $1 bills and spend them freely on bottles of water.

Be prepared to feel like some holy sites would be holier with fewer people. (Most of us know the feeling of the church getting in the way of our worship.)

Recognize that some historical sites are a bit sketchy. A multitude of signs point sightseers to "David's Tomb." The first thing the guide says is, "We are certain this is not David's tomb." I assume they found that "Not David's Tomb" did not draw many tourists.

Leave your skepticism at home. The Church of the Nativity is probably not on the exact spot of Jesus' birth. That does not change the sacred truth that pilgrims have been coming to that spot for almost 1,700 years to give thanks for Jesus' coming. Just get in line.

Be grateful for sites that are more likely. The well in Nazareth has been the only well in town since long before the time of Jesus. If Mary and Joseph went to a well, it was the one I saw (though, admittedly, it did not have a big church on top of it).

Most places where there is any chance a particular biblical story took place are marked with churches. I did not see "The Church of the Head of John the Baptist on a Platter," but I would not have been surprised.

Write down the names of churches you see, in case you are ever starting a church and want something out of the ordinary. Have you seen any of these in your town: The Church of the Adolescent Jesus, The Church of the Flagellation or The Church of Our Lady of the Spasm?

Float in the Dead Sea if you must, but do not expect to enjoy it. It is basically a bath in poisoned baby oil.

You will quickly recognize that when the Bible says Jesus went to the wilderness, it was easy — because 99% of the country is wilderness. Do not, however, ask your guide born in Israel if the person who first called this "the land flowing with milk and honey" was being sarcastic. He will not be amused.

Don't expect camel rides or belly dancers, but take a camera anyway.

Enjoy the exotic foods. I started my trip looking forward to falafel, shawarma, and the fish's head being left on. By the end, I was looking for McDonald's.

Make your way through the crowd, kneel and push a list of prayer concerns into a crack in the Wailing Wall. It couldn't hurt.

Sit on the beach where the resurrected Jesus served the disciples the Lord's breakfast. Wish you could have been there, and then realize that you are.

Get baptized in the Jordan River — even though you have to walk through Disneyland to get there. You still might feel a little of what Jesus felt.

Pray through the Beatitudes while sitting on the Mount of the Beatitudes. Read about Jesus' birth while you are at the Shepherds' Field in Bethlehem, the stilling of the storm while on a boat on the Sea of Galilee, Zacchaeus while standing beneath the oldest sycamore tree in Jericho, and Peter's denial while in the courtyard where it happened. Walk the Via Dolorosa, the way of suffering, and marvel at Jesus' courage.

The best stories are often about people traveling far from home to discover that what they most need was at home all the time. A Catholic priest welcomed our group by saying that he hoped we were not there as religious tourists, but had come to "meet the Risen Christ." We could have responded that we believe we can meet Christ every day — no matter where we are. Sometimes the treasure we go looking for has been with us all along.

A preacher goes parrothead
August 2008

The church is supposed to teach the world about joy, and it often works that way. But at times it happens in the other direction.

Some church members decided that Carol and I needed a break — the kind that lasts about three hours — and bought us tickets to a Jimmy Buffett concert. We didn't want to be rude, so we went. Their gift was even more generous than you might guess, because we ended up in the middle section not far from Jimmy. I admit I wouldn't want Jimmy Buffett to teach my son's Sunday school class, but it was fun.

Jimmy is a balding 60-year-old. The theme for this tour is "The Year of Still Here." If you're Jimmy Buffett — who's crashed planes and boats — still being around is an accomplishment.

The band is made up of graying AARP members with artificial knees and orthopedic shoes who have been with the band forever and never make it on to the jumbotron, along with a couple of dancers in their 20s who get lots of jumbotron time.

You get the feeling that most of the crowd has been to these concerts before. For one thing, they dress for the event. Grown-ups wear parrot noses, parrot heads, shark fins, straw hats, flowered shirts, hula skirts and pirate suits. Several were carrying swords, and a few had surfboards. I saw a 35-foot sailboat in the parking lot. What were they thinking?

Jimmy made several references to religion. He claimed that the pope came to his concert in Houston, blessed the cheeseburgers (a Buffett reference) and told Jimmy he had long been a parrothead.

Jimmy also said: "Church attendance might be down in the morning, but for those worried about that, well, for me, this counts as church."

It doesn't count for church. Carol and I made it to church the next morning, but there were moments Saturday night that were joyful in ways that the church should be joyful.

The concert was meant to be fun, and it was. It was like being at the beach without the irritating sun, sand and water. People want to feel joyful and are willing to work at it.

I found one element especially interesting — the beach balls. At any given moment, hundreds of beach balls were flying through the air. Sitting near the front down on the field meant we had more beach ball action than people 50 rows up the bleachers. One beach ball caused Carol to spill much of her $5 Dr Pepper.

What I enjoyed most about the beach balls was thinking about how they got there. Hundreds of people thought, "I like it when we throw beach balls, so I'll stop and buy one on the way to the concert." They do this knowing there is not a chance in a thousand that they will be bringing their beach ball home. Once they launch it, it's not coming back. They are making a contribution to the party.

Here's my point — and you may be surprised to hear I have one. Church is supposed to be about gathering to make a contribution to the party. In the Old Testament, one third of the tithes that were given at the temple went for feast days. Think about that: 33% of their budget went for parties. They believed that those who love God should give thanks and celebrate.

Sometimes we try so hard to make everyone think like we do that we miss the fun of church. We plan. We program. We process. We work. We worry. We argue. We disagree. At times, we bring our most disagreeable self to church.

We don't celebrate enough. We don't laugh enough. We need to sing and smile and give thanks to God that we're still here.

Breakfast in Peppertown
February 2011

Don't tell my mom. She won't understand. When I was growing up, we did not eat out. I have no childhood memories of restaurants. Diners were as off-limits as pool halls, casinos and Methodist churches. Eating out was morally dubious.

My mother's questions were unanswerable: "Why do you want to waste our money? Is there something wrong with my cooking? Do you think Jesus went out to eat when Mary had supper on the table?"

You might think "We love your cooking, just like Jesus would, and want to show our gratitude by giving you a break" would be a reasonable argument. You would be wrong.

When we went on vacation, mom packed bologna sandwiches, so I got used to driving past Dairy Queens. But there was one eatery that I continued to look at with unrequited longing.

Peppertown Restaurant is at the intersection of County Road 383 and County Road 178, five miles and six Baptist churches from my parents' house. Every time we drove past I imagined the haute cuisine they must be serving. I pictured my favorite foods prepared with astonishing flair. The chef would grace the table with surprisingly inventive bologna sandwiches. I could hear welcoming voices: "Brett, we haven't seen you in here before, but we knew you would make it eventually." Peppertown Restaurant was my vision of the heavenly banquet.

I told my mother we would not be getting to her house until 2:30, so she shouldn't wait on us for lunch — especially since lunch is now at 10:30. At 2:00 when we drove past the PR I surreptitiously decided it would be the last time I passed the extravagant café without having tasted the forbidden fruit. At 2:15, lunch was waiting on my mom's table. She served pot roast, mashed potatoes, green bean casserole, yeast rolls and two kinds of pie — pecan and lemon ice box.

I gained five pounds, but we had a nice visit. I read the *Tupelo Daily Journal* each morning, played touch football and worked on a 1,000-piece puzzle (it was a snow scene with white clouds, so we felt okay getting only about 400 together). We successfully avoided subjects that have given us trouble in the past — the current president, the last president, public schools, women ministers, gay people, Jonah's completely literal whale, Japanese cars, movies not starring John Wayne, and the Dallas Cowboys.

On the night before we were to leave, I told my mom that we wouldn't be able to stay for breakfast. I chose not to reveal my rebellious plan. The next morning, after almost 50 years of passing by, I stopped. Ours was the only car that was not a truck. We almost parked in front of a "The Last Car That Parked Here is Still Missing" notice. My heart was pounding as I opened the door. At the counter we briefly considered "Push here for service," but the button is set on a mousetrap. Everyone was friendly: "Just grab a table. There's a nice one in the back next to the heater." It was the friendliness that ushers offer people who clearly have not been to church before.

There is a fine line between antiques and old junk. The Peppertown Restaurant is filled with signs that could go either way: Hostess Creme-filled Twinkies 10¢, Buy Pepsi-Cola Today 5¢, Hot Dogs 15¢, and "Chewing allowed, Spitting ain't." I so wished the photograph of Elvis, who was born about 10 miles from there, had been taken at the PR, but it wasn't.

We were in one of the few remaining places where Mississippians assume that everyone not from Mississippi has an accent. I was a little thrown by the girl wearing the "I ♥ NY" T-shirt that would have been frowned upon not many years ago. She was trying to explain Facebook to her grandfather. "Preacher man," in an orange cap and camouflage, held court near the front. A couple prayed quietly over their breakfast.

If it had been lunchtime, I would have ordered the sweet tater fries. The butter biscuit sounded good and the chocolate biscuits tempting. I almost ordered the bologna biscuit — which I had long dreamed would be there — but at the last minute I switched to fried eggs and toast. The coffee came in only one flavor, but I had both grape and strawberry jelly. The eggs were just the right level of crispy. Breakfast tasted like the extravagance my upbringing taught me to fear. Maybe it is time I visit a Methodist church.

Bread of heaven
October 2011

I have never been on a spiritual pilgrimage to St. Peter's Basilica in Rome, Our Lady of Lourdes in France or the Precious Moments Chapel in Carthage, Mo., but I have experienced the International Biscuit Festival in Knoxville, Tenn. Fifteen thousand biscuit (15,000) lovers responded to the invitation to "get our biscuit on." Each one understood that "biscuits" is the perfect way to end the sentence, "Pass the …"

The purpose of art exhibitions is to teach us to pay attention to the grandeur of the ordinary world, but the International Biscuit Festival points to the grandeur of an otherworldly experience. The festival celebrates the gathering of flour, salt, butter, milk and baking powder into God's most perfect food.

Biscuit Boulevard was filled with big tents and gingham-covered tables. The greeters' name tags implored us, "Ask me about my biscuits." What do biscuit evangelists do with these T-shirts the rest of the year?

> *Man cannot live by biscuits alone, but it's fun to try*
> *I'm soft, fluffy and warm on the inside*
> *BYOB — Butter Your Own Biscuits*
> *Life is a biscuit*
> *Biscuit in the oven*

The tasting area was two blocks of flaky heaven. If you are picturing biscuits from Hardee's, Chick-fil-A or McDonald's with a slab of sausage in the middle, you are a biscuit beginner. Neither are these your grandmother's biscuits — even if they were wonderful.

Twenty gastronomic geniuses brought their signature biscuits. The University of Tennessee Culinary Institute had, appropriately, an orange and yellow biscuit. Callie's Charleston Pimento Cheese Biscuit claimed to be Oprah's favorite. We enjoyed pizza biscuits, chocolate biscuits, sweet potato casserole biscuits, blueberry and jalapeno biscuits, barbecue biscuits with tomato jam and smoked cheddar, apple butter biscuits with honey and cinnamon, and Rheem bologna German blue cheese brie biscuits. One restaurant served gluten-free biscuits. (We need to care for those with serious allergies, but gluten — whatever it is — sounds like a crucial ingredient in biscuits. This may be like decaf coffee — what's the point?)

Last year's winning biscuit was an Elvis biscuit with — you guessed it — peanut butter and banana. This year's winner was Café 4's entry — an orange cranberry streusel biscuit that featured a zesty cream cheese center. Early on we stopped asking, "What kind of biscuits do we want?" and asked only "Why would we turn down any biscuit?"

We did not arrive in time for the "Pre-heat Show," but we caught several acts from The Sweet Tea Tour. I am disappointed that we missed hearing the Black Bottom Biscuits. (Limp Bizkit must not have been invited.)

My favorite event was the Miss and Mr. Biscuit Pageant. We had the good fortune of sitting behind Miss Biscuit 2010. She shouted encouraging comments to this year's contestants: "Work that apron." More interesting were the disparaging remarks she whispered about this year's contestants: "What a Pillsbury Dough Boy he is." Biscuit pageants are cut throat.

I liked the poem that began "The air was cool. The oven was hot." But some of the poetry was not the best: "I love biscuits more than my life. I'd like to have a biscuit for my wife." Neither of these contestants won. The judges were not swayed by the contestant who tossed flying biscuits into the crowd. Miss Biscuit 2011 Sara Quall earned the judges' favor with biscuit song stylings. Her spirited rap number began, "I like big biscuits I cannot lie." (In the midst of big biscuits it was appropriate that the festival raised funds for Second Harvest to eliminate childhood hunger.)

The intellectual aspects of biscuits were not overlooked. Barnes and Noble's tent was filled with biscuit literature: *You're the Butter on My Biscuit*, *Butter My Butt and Call Me a Biscuit*, and *Bon Appétit Y'all*. If Borders had a larger biscuit section, they would still be in business.

I looked for *Biscuits in the Bible*, but surprisingly it was not there. How have scholars missed this rich area of study? The Bible mentions what could be translated biscuits many times. The manna from heaven might be biscuits. At the feeding of the five thousand, Philip finds a boy with five fish and what may be two biscuits. Surely some Southern scholar has argued that there were biscuits at the Lord's Supper.

The one who said "I am the Bread of Life" must love this festival and the great variety of people who shared what felt a little like dinner on the grounds and a little like Communion. Is it too much to suggest that biscuits can be an essential ingredient in our Christian discipleship? Biscuits help us follow the command in the Psalms to "Taste and see that God is good."

Getting our ducks in a row
August 2002

Donald Duck, Daisy Duck, Huey, Dewey and Louie Duck, Daffy Duck, Peking ducks, Oregon Ducks, Mighty Ducks, duct tape and Duck Soup are fine ducks. They're good ducks, great ducks, even Hall of Fame ducks (like Joe "Ducky" Medwick, St. Louis Cardinals outfielder), but only in their dreams did they get to be Peabody Ducks. My family was privileged to see the world-famous Peabody Ducks.

Since the 1930s, every morning at 11:00 the ducks come down the elevator and march into the lobby of the Peabody Hotel in Memphis, Tenn. Children and adults come from all over the world to take a gander. Well-dressed people sipping from $80 bottles of French wine line the red carpet and hang from the balcony to clap and cheer as the ducks process to the music of John Phillip Sousa. On Friday morning at 10:55, as we waited with joyous anticipation, our camera at the ready, I overhead this conversation:

"This is stupid. They're ducks."

"You're stupid! They're Peabody Ducks!"

The ducks swim happily in the fountain all day long. They've heard the announcer explain countless times that the fountain's centerpiece is made from one piece of Italian marble. Cherubs hold up a bowl of brightly colored flowers.

At precisely 5:00 in the afternoon, the duckmaster returns dressed in his top hat, whistles and medals (doubtless earned with great valor). The ducks march out of the lobby, into the elevator, and up to the roof where they spend the evening in their Victorian duck palace.

Most ducks walk with a kind of casual silliness, their short necks and legs bouncing happily. A Peabody duck moves with regal elegance. It's a walk that says trouble must fall away like water off a duck's back. Whether the rain falls or the sun shines, it's a good day for the ducks.

It's also a good day for the keepers of the ducks. The Lucky Duck gift shop in the lobby of the Peabody does a brisk business selling duck umbrellas, duck earrings, duck slippers, duck bill holders, rubber duckies, stuffed ducks (not dead ducks, 100% polyester), Santa ducks (1/2 price) and Elvis ducks (it's Memphis).

If it looks like a duck, walks like a duck and quacks like a duck, it's probably a duck — unless it's a Peabody. There are no ugly ducklings in this family. The Peabodys are Rockefellers, Carnegies and Kennedys. It's easy to imagine that when their heads hit their goose down pillows, they pray: "Thank you, Lord, for my good luck and for making me a Peabody Duck."

As you have realized, I've been thinking about this way too much. At first glance it seems that life is just ducky for Peabody Ducks. Who wouldn't want to live in a plush penthouse? Who wouldn't want their duck prints on the sidewalk in front of the hotel? Who wouldn't want a life of luxury?

And yet, is it possible that Peabody Ducks are missing out? What if, after a while, ducks cease to be impressed by chandeliers, the grand piano, and splashing in the same fountain, even one carved from Italian marble, every day? What if they feel like sitting ducks? Maybe as they line up for the Sousa march they wish they weren't just another duck in a row. What if the duckiest life is seeing new sights, finding long-forgotten lakes, and heading into the wild blue yonder? Why would you want to waddle, even on a red carpet, when you can fly?

Me and the Boss
June 2008

I was 14 years old when Bruce Springsteen released the *Born to Run* album — though for me it was the *Born to Run* 8-track. The player in my 1969 Chevy Impala eventually required a Popsicle stick to adjust the tracking, because I wore it out listening to those eight songs over and over. I sang duets with the Boss in the car and never in the house, because I knew that the requisite volume as well as the lyrics would not go over big. I couldn't see my mother singing along to: "Someday girl I don't know when we're gonna' get to that place where we really want to go and we'll walk in the sun, but till then tramps like us baby we were born to run."

When Bruce and the E Street Band came to Cleveland, a friend said: "A bunch of us are going to hear Springsteen. Do you want to go?"

Most aficionados would have immediately, enthusiastically shouted, "Yes!" but most aficionados weren't conservative-leaning-to-fundamentalist-Southern-Baptists. I ended up saying "No," because I was secretly afraid of the people who would be there. The friend who invited me wasn't one of my church friends. I pictured a crowd drinking beer and smoking dope. My religious upbringing made it clear that I shouldn't be part of a mob of criminals, reprobates and good-for-nothings. (I was also taught to stay away from black people, poor people and loose women.)

But I've kept listening and singing along. The lullaby to which I put my children to sleep began, "In the day we sweat it out in the streets of a runaway American dream" and ended, "Baby we were born to run."

When Bruce came to Dallas a few weeks ago, I decided with some trepidation to join the mob. When we got in line, I started scribbling a few ideas.

A grandmother in a bandana asked, "What are you writing?"
I answered, "I'm a Baptist minister taking notes for a column."
I don't think she believed me.

When we got to our seats — which were "backstage" but not in a good way — the balding man to my right, who ended up knowing more of the words than I did, looked at me and said, "Some of this crowd would fit right in at a Perry Como concert."

The could-have-been-a-vice-principal woman next to Carol asked, "Do you think we'll have to stand through this?"

A quick glance at the gray hair around us made Carol confident in saying, "I'm sure we'll get to sit."

Some stood for the whole two and a half hours. Some danced in the aisles. We clapped and raised our hands. We shouted and sang as a congregation. It felt like a Pentecostal revival.

Bruce led us in a hymn about people who might not make it to church, but keep believing.

In a whitewash shotgun shack an old man passes away
Take his body to the graveyard and over him they pray
Lord won't you tell us, tell us what does it mean
Still at the end of every hard-earned day people find some
reason to believe.

The Boss thinks we're all in this together — criminals, reprobates and church people:

Everybody needs a place to rest
Everybody wants to have a home
Don't make no difference what nobody says
Ain't nobody likes to be alone.
Everybody's got a hungry heart.

I looked at the people who were singing with such joy and was embarrassed for myself and for the part of the church that keeps pushing people away. The choir included drinkers and teetotalers, the promiscuous and the chaste, black and white, old and young, bikers and Baptists preachers. Where in the Gospels do any of us get the idea that church people should feel superior to anyone else in the crowd?

I was 33 years late to the concert, but I'm beginning to understand that God loves us all — even the tramps like us that were born to run.

Up in the air
November 2011

I now know all about flying between Atlanta and Wilmington, N.C., thanks to the gracious people at First Baptist Church, where I am serving as the interim preacher. This column is just a small percentage of what I know.

Soaring 30,000 feet above your problems makes your problems seem small. This dreamy feeling lasts about five minutes.

From my house to Parking Lot A, it is exactly 33 miles unless you forget that the sign directing you to parking says "Rental Car." Put your parking ticket over the driver's side visor carefully. If your ticket somehow makes its way under the seat, it may take a while to find it. Write precisely where your car is parked on the back of the Park 'n' Ride ticket. "Between two trucks" may not be helpful two days later.

You are not expected to tip the shuttle driver unless he or she carries your bags. This is why you keep your bags close to you. Do not say, "I was pretty cute that day," as the security officer checks your photo I.D. These people are not easily amused. On the flight from Atlanta, leave yourself 30 minutes for security and the train to your concourse. On the flight from Wilmington, you can get to the airport five minutes before your flight.

Do not go to the security line on the far right in Atlanta. If they don't have enough people to fill the "suspicious looking characters" line, you may end up with your hands over your head in an X-ray booth that was featured in several episodes of *Star Trek*. SkyMiles Club members (I'm only 75,000 miles or 150 trips to Wilmington from Platinum status) know that the TSA doesn't really care if you keep your belt on, but your shoes are still a big deal. Efficient travelers roll our eyes at people who don't know how much three ounces is.

The attendant at Gate D40 is the best: "I've got 300 Delta dollars for someone who loves their mother. You can be slightly inconvenienced today and visit your mother for free at Thanksgiving. What kind of ungrateful child wouldn't do that?"

"We're boarding zones one and two" is an invitation for passengers in zone three. Most travelers believe that any bag will go into the overhead bin if you push hard enough. Go for the aisle seats. Seat assignments are more suggestions than assignments — especially if there's a baby on board. (Most babies prefer traveling on Saturdays.) In much the same way, flight times are guidelines rather than genuine commitments on the part of the airlines.

The plane to Wilmington is not a 747 or even in the 700 Club. Sometimes we see geese pass. Passengers can be impatient. Twenty minutes on the tarmac is like two hours anywhere else. Frequent flyers are efficient people, but we know we'll get there when we get there and with free peanuts.

Like most travelers, I no longer expect to be surprised. But on a recent trip back to Atlanta, a tiny Hispanic woman hesitantly got on the train to the main terminal. She seemed confused, but I worried that a SkyMiles member asking, "Do you know where you're going?" would seem condescending. She was trying to read the rapidly scrolling directions (which I think are in French half of the time). Finally she asked, "Is this to pick up suitcases?"

She was not speaking in her first language — which puts her at least one language ahead of me.

I explained: "You want the fifth stop — after C, B, A and T. You want baggage claim. That's the last stop. I'll be getting off there. I'll show you."

When we got to T, she nervously asked, "Are you sure?"

"Yes, we'll get off at the next stop and go to the escalator on the right. When we get to the top we'll take a left to baggage claim. Was this your first flight?"

She nodded, "Yes."

When we got to the top of the escalator she didn't need my help any more. Two girls about six and eight screamed as they waved their "Welcome Home, Mom!" poster. Dad beamed. Mom cried. The four of them danced and hugged. They were joyful, delighted and ecstatic. I wasn't the only one who stopped to watch. Several travelers who had spent most of the day looking at their watches finally thought about something genuinely important. Efficiency isn't much of a goal.

Leftovers

Dancing with the devil
November 2007

When I was growing up, every ethical question had one indisputable answer. It was abundantly clear, for example, that dancing of any sort was a sin for which we should not bank on forgiveness. Two-stepping was the fast lane on the road to perdition. This zero-tolerance policy was not to be questioned. We divided the good people from the bad by how much they moved when they listened to George Jones.

When I was in high school I remember Susan Alexander and her mother coming to speak to my father, their pastor, about an important matter. Susan wanted to go to a school dance. She explained that she understood the evils of dancing and would not under any circumstances dance, but she would like to attend to be a witness, to show that Christians can have fun without dancing.

Illustration by Scott Brooks

Susan's mother did not share this view. She felt that the Bible was clear on "Shun from every appearance of evil" and if God had believed there should be an exception for high school dances, God would have written it in. My father didn't hesitate. "Susan, if you're not going to Baltimore, why do you want to go to the train station?"

In 1979, my freshman year at Baylor, I was part of a backyard Bible club that met at Good Samaritan Baptist Church in East Waco. Every Tuesday we told Bible stories and played with about 30 children. After about a month the leader of our Bible club, whom I considered a saint, suggested the workers, eight Baylor students, needed to get to know each other.

Kimberly Smith, a junior I thought was a decent person, said, "I know. Let's go kicker dancing." My jaw dropped, but I assumed the others would reply, "No, we don't think we'll be spending a Saturday night on hell's doorstep warming ourselves in the flames though it's certainly interesting that you would suggest it."

But to my horror the other six, including the saint, nodded their heads in agreement and said — and this disgusted me — "Sounds like fun."

I assumed these people weren't going to Baltimore, but they were planning to get on the train.

You might wonder why I didn't say, "I'm not sure that a trip to a honky tonk where there will be cussing, smoking and drinking as well as dancing is appropriate for a Bible club." I expected to hear myself shout, "Stop the train" any second, but I didn't. Some mysterious power held me back.

All week I felt like Caesar deciding whether or not to cross the Rubicon. Somehow I knew that if I did I could never go back. After five days of wrestling with an angel or a demon, on Saturday night I learned several things. I learned that I cannot dance, but it's not because of religious reasons. My rhythm gene is not just underused or defective, but completely missing. I discovered that "Cotton-Eyed Joe" — which is what the band at the West Fraternal Auditorium made every song sound like — will never be my favorite song. I learned that I will always be rethinking what's sinful and what isn't.

We had a dance at our church not long ago, and I saw a woman who looked just like Susan Alexander's mother.

Temptation's surprising appearance
May 2002

Growing up, my parents and my church and most of my friends called themselves Baptist, but in reality we were — in most of the ways that mattered to a teenager — Amish.

We not only didn't drink or sleep around, but we didn't personally know anyone who did. We saw those people. They went to the Piggly Wiggly — the grocery store that sold beer. Everyone at my church went to Jitney Jungle — I'm not making these names up — because they didn't sell beer.

We knew where the pool hall was, where most of the drinking in town reportedly took place, but no one in my youth group had ever been there. Not only had alcohol never passed my lips, but I had never seen it pass anyone else's lips either.

In much the same way, we knew there were 17-year-olds who slept around, but we didn't know any of them — though I tended to imagine such 17-year-old girls. I imagined these women wore bright red dresses or tight-fitting blue jeans. They had long painted fingernails and were always looking for young Baptist/Amish victims to lure into depravity. The Amish kids were less sheltered than I was.

Before I went to Baylor, a deacon who was shocked that I was going someplace more worldly than Criswell Bible Institute pulled me aside and said, "When you get to college, you will face temptations you have never imagined. There will be hard-drinking, loose-living women. You need to decide right now that you will have nothing to do with them, because if the devil gets hold of you she doesn't let go."

So as a freshman I was constantly on the lookout out for wild women with drinking problems, but I couldn't find any. So after a while I let my guard down. While taking Introduction to New Testament, I was distracted by a Lutheran pastor's daughter who sat right in front of me. Yvonne was attractive enough to frighten me, but she seemed like a nice person. After a couple of weeks she said "hi" and I said "hi."

I was thrilled that we were hitting it off. After a couple more weeks of waiting for her to say hi again, I finally asked her if she would like to go out to eat and to a G-rated movie. We went to Monterrey House, a nice family restaurant. We talked about our churches and how wonderful it is to be a preacher's kid, but when our food came, she said — and I'll never forget this, no matter how hard I try — "Isn't it strange to have Mexican food without beer?" I tried to keep breathing, but I couldn't. Where I grew up, she might as well have said, "Isn't it strange to eat enchiladas without crack cocaine sprinkled on top?" or "Isn't it strange to have tacos without small children as an appetizer?"

I realized who she was. She was temptation. The devil had finally arrived, and she was wearing blue jeans. She was a hard-drinking, loose-living woman planning to lure me into the depravity I had been warned about.

I spent the rest of the evening terrified, but apparently she recognized my spiritual strength, and the invisible armor of God I was wearing, and made no further attempts to steal my soul.

What I've learned since then, much to my disappointment, is that for most of us temptation doesn't wear a red dress or tight-fitting blue jeans. It's not usually flashy or frightening or obvious. The temptations that are most likely to steal our souls are quiet and often boring. They are the temptations to be dull and apathetic, and they are more dangerous than I ever imagined.

Life's laundry list
October 2001

Books on the spiritual disciplines include chapters on prayer, Scripture, worship, fasting, meditation and so on, but they usually make a glaring omission. The most neglected spiritual practice, by far, is laundry. In Exodus 19:10, "The Lord said unto Moses, Go unto the people and sanctify them today and tomorrow, and let them wash their clothes." It's no coincidence that angels are usually pictured in "bright," which might be translated "just out of the dryer," clothing. When John Wesley said "Cleanliness is next to godliness," he was on to a vital truth.

As with other spiritual disciplines, we are tempted to let initial failures keep us from trying again. We don't like to talk about it, but most of us have had bad experiences with reds and whites that became pinks. Those disappointments, which may have come while we were still immature in our faith, should not lead us to say, "I'm no spiritual giant. Laundry's not for me." We need to ask, "What are the keys to growing spiritually through laundry?"

Simplicity is crucial. Avoid products with names such as the "Wonder Washing Disc." Don't give much attention to fancy fabric softeners, starch, bleach, and ironing. Use less detergent than the powers-that-be tell you to use. Laundry that deepens our journey is straightforward washing in the normal cycle with no frills.

Sorting is a way of appreciating the diversity within creation. Spirituality is free, but it's also ordered, so read labels. Recognize the difference between permanent press and delicate, but don't see that difference as a negative; it's a gift. Sort carefully, but every once in a while playfully toss a pair of old white socks into a blue load just to see what happens. Wash in all temperatures, but use hot only when absolutely necessary. When you spray a tough greasy spot with stain remover, think about what the prophet Jeremiah said: "For though thou wash thee with nitre, and take thee with much soap, yet thine iniquity is marked" (2:22). Be glad that you have a can of Shout instead of nitre.

Laundry and spirituality take time. Don't be in a hurry. Wisdom knows that two minutes in the spin cycle saves 20 in the dryer. Be still and listen to the washer making the world cleaner. Fold in quiet reflection. Try not to think too much when you're folding. I used to mistakenly ask, "Why do I wash the towels so much? Aren't we clean when we use them?"

When you hang shirts, realize that you are stating your hope in the future. Pairing socks is an act of reconciliation, but don't worry when a sock escapes from the dryer. It will find its place. Remember that it's not the clothes that make the man (or woman); it's folding the clothes. Don't live every day as if it's your last — or you'll never wash clothes.

Doing someone else's laundry is an expression of agapé love. Though folding is usually a time for solitude, it must also to be taught to and shared with children. Begin with age-appropriate folding. Don't give your 5-year-old a fitted sheet; it's cruel (though undeniably amusing). Some people find meaning in praying as they fold: "Thank you for the socks that will cover my feet. Where should my feet take me tomorrow?" If you pray over your laundry, do so silently. If someone hears and expresses admiration for your spirituality, you may become proud.

In his farewell speech to the Hebrew people (Deut. 29:5) Moses said, "I have led you forty years in the wilderness; your clothes are not waxen upon you." We should be grateful for our non-waxen (clean) clothes. In Revelation 7:14, the ones who come through the tribulation "have washed their robes." The people who do laundry, who are "clothed with righteousness" live deeper, fuller lives.

In his 17th century classic of Christian devotion, *The Practice of the Presence of God*, Brother Lawrence tells of discovering God while washing pots and pans: "I possess God as peacefully in the bustle of my kitchen, as I do upon my knees before the Holy Sacrament. My faith becomes enlightened. It seems to me that the curtain of obscurity is drawn, and that the endless cloudless day of the other life is dawning." We can only imagine how enlightened he would have been if, instead of the kitchen, he had been in charge of the laundry.

Scrubbing the tub
April 2008

I like washing dishes. I like clearing, sudsing, rinsing and the threat of a spoon sneaking into the disposal. I like stubborn cheese graters. I like having enough engineering skills to fit the last pan into the dishwasher. Lots of people who love to eat love to cook, but a few of us love to wash dishes.

I like doing laundry. I like dividing permanent press from delicate. I like running "air fluff" just for fun. I like to believe that pairing socks is an act of reconciliation and washing clothes is an investment in the future.

I've never seen my father rinse a coffee cup or hang a dress shirt. He's a good person, but I doubt he knows the location of the dishwasher tabs or the lint filter. Because I do dishes and wash clothes, I think of myself as a good husband. I enjoy patting myself on the back for my forays into cleaning.

But every once in a while my beloved points out that my progress as a housekeeper hasn't been as impressive as I like to think. I don't iron, mop or dust. I don't scrub the tub, clean the toilet or wash windows. I like to think this is a matter of focusing on my strengths — dishes and clothes — but it's really about my unwillingness to do something harder.

Most church people like going to worship. We like signing our name on the friendship register. We like standing when there's an asterisk and reading the bold print. We like singing hymns and knowing to look carefully at the words of the Doxology, because they might change. We like recognizing the organ dismissal.

Most church people are genuinely nice. We like being kind to the people who are kind to us. We like being friendly to our friends and to those who look like they might become friends.

We like being good neighbors and careful drivers. We like being nice people.

We know people who don't go to church and who aren't nice. (Some of them are our relatives.) They don't know how to act in church and drive too fast. Because we are nicer than most people, we are tempted to pat ourselves on the back for being good churchgoers.

But every once in a while God reminds us there is more. We can learn how better to welcome the stranger, invite a friend to be part of the church, ask a homeless woman to tell her story, share a hurting family's sorrow, read the Bible with an openness to being wrong, and pray asking God to change us into more of who we should be.

Churches get used to the routine — washing the dishes and doing the laundry of religious expectations. It's easier to have church than it is to be church. We are tempted to pat ourselves on the back for the depth of our understanding and the generosity of our ministries, but God is always calling us to more.

We need to consider the hard things God may be calling us to do. I'm going to think about it while I'm scrubbing the tub.

The joy of sox
May 2006

Most biblical scholars neglect to point out how prominent footwear is in scripture. In Ezekiel 16:10, the prophet predicts $200 tennis shoes: "I clothed thee also with broidered work, and shod thee with badgers' skin, and girded thee about with fine linen, and I covered thee with silk."

The name of Jacob, one of Israel's patriarchs, means "one who grabs the heel" — which could be paraphrased "one who grabs the sock."

A common punishment was being forced to go without shoes and socks (and in Isaiah 20:2 everything else as well): "Put off thy shoe from thy foot. And he did so, walking naked and barefoot."

God guards the faithful's toes: "God will keep the feet of the saints" (1 Sam. 2:9).

Ministers' feet are especially striking: "How beautiful are the feet of those that preach the gospel of peace" (Rom. 10:15).

During a recent sermon, while making insightful comments about how our desires change as we grow older and without being aware that I was walking on holy ground, I said: "This is my birthday, so my family has been asking, 'What do you want?' It took a while, but I finally came up with three requests: 1. To have the leaves raked. This was also my Christmas gift. 2. Six pairs of identical black dress socks. That way if you lose one, you're still in business. 3. Six pairs of white athletic socks with blue stripes so that they can be identified when another member of my family 'borrows' them."

Two days later our church's Tuesday crowd — a Bible study and the International Ministry — socked it to me. They gave me a huge basket of fine-quality hosiery, 105 pairs of socks. (Our minister of education has already asked to preach just before his birthday.) I was told to buy a blue marker if I wanted stripes, but I got everything else you can imagine in a sock. I have socks with red stripes and longer lasting heels. I received premium rib, cushion crew, relaxed fit tube and Lycra Powerfit socks for intense training. I have socks with padding at the toes for added comfort. My new socks have breathability, durability and gold toes. I have socks designed by Ralph Lauren and socks from Big Lots.

I now know everything you always wanted to know about socks, but were afraid to ask.

I received socks with guarantees: "If you are not satisfied with this product, launder and return it to Consumer Relations, Box 26535, Greensboro, N.C., and we will gladly replace it." (Laundering seems like a reasonable requirement.)

My favorite is a pair of knitted socks with a note that said, "I had not knitted a pair of socks in 58 years, because in 1948 when I was a junior in high school, I dated a boy who wanted a pair of hand-knit argyle socks, and I did knit them, and he wore them faithfully at least once a week, until the summer when he attended a church camp and committed himself to God and came home and broke up with me, because he was going to be a minister and he said I wouldn't be a good preacher's wife."

I can understand why Alice didn't knit a sock for 58 years, but I've assured her there's a church somewhere with an idiot for their pastor.

It was made clear to me that our church's clothing room ministry would be expecting a large donation from me very soon. Almost all of the socks have made it to our Baptist Center, but I loved having the basket in my office for a couple of days. I can't remember a more clever, delightful and helpful gift.

Our clothing room gives one pair of socks per person per month. Socks are especially important for those who are homeless and have to walk everywhere. By the time you read this, 105 people who really need them will have cleaner, warmer socks.

Churches need to find wonderful, funny, creative ways to care for those who need our help. I may ask for shoes next year.

Shoe business
January 2007

Every five years or so, whether I need to or not, I go to the cheapest shoe store I can find to buy a new pair of everyday shoes. My old pair was beyond old. I avoided puddles with my left foot because of the hole in the sole. The insoles were missing, so they slipped up and down like flip-flops.

When I told Carol it was time for new shoes, she sent Caleb along to buy tennis shoes. I was confused when he stayed in the aisle where I was until I realized that my 12-year-old now shares my shoe size. Caleb also picks shoes by the same criteria — the first ones we try on with which we can live. He quickly selected midnight navy/metallic silver — Overplay Nikes that cost more than all the Keds I ever wore.

I asked the cobbler for dull, brown, everyday shoes with strings, but apparently they don't make those anymore. The first shoes he found were peculiar. They looked like moccasins with rubber stops on the back of the heels. They were a poor man's penny loafers with no place for the penny. They were the opposite of the blue suede shoes Elvis didn't want stepped on, but they were dull, brown, on sale and shamefully comfortable. Dr. Scholl's Memory Fit Insoles are like walking on marshmallows. I knew they weren't fashionable, but these were the kind of comfy shoes an old woman with many children might want to live in.

Carol wasn't impressed with my purchase.

"You bought house shoes."

"I did not."

"You did so."

She had a point. They look and feel like house shoes. On Monday morning I almost put them back in the closet but then thought, "Maybe nobody will notice."

Nobody noticed. I should have been wearing house shoes for years.

On Tuesday I asked Pat Smith, one of the church secretaries, what she thought of my new shoes. She looked puzzled, "Why did you buy driving shoes?"

I'm going to keep wearing my driving shoes/moccasins/house shoes, because I've decided that my feet don't deserve to be pinched by acceptable shoes.

We do way too much for the sake of appearances. (The devil makes people wear Prada.) Looking good is exhausting — or so I've heard.

People spend their lives doing what seems respectable. Some lawyers would live with more joy if they were kindergarten teachers. Some wives who drive a Lexus would be happier if they had waited for the guy who drives a Yugo.

Some of the people at the opera would rather be at the ballgame. Some at the ballgame would rather be at the library. Some reading the *Wall Street Journal* would rather be reading the Psalms. Some eating at a fancy French restaurant would really enjoy a burger and fries.

We run errands that don't need to be run. We go to events that aren't worth our time. We buy gifts to impress people who don't need our gifts.

What looks good to the rest of the world may not be the way to go. We should spend less time worrying what others think and more time looking for what leads to real joy.

Most resolutions are completely unreasonable: "I will never raise my voice again." "I will read a book every day." "I will lose a pound a week for the rest of my life."

Consider this resolution: I will do what makes my feet want to dance.

Shaved by grace
July 2009

Christians cannot avoid difficult ethical issues such as materialism, militarism and mustaches. That last one has been on my mind and face lately.

I stopped shaving and a week later when Carol noticed she surprised me, "It looks good."

Another visually impaired friend commented, "It gives you an edge."

I can use an edge, so I put my razor away.

I wanted my beard to be reminiscent of some famous historical figure — Abraham Lincoln, Sigmund Freud or Albus Dumbledore. Unfortunately, my beard makes me look like Al Gore, Shaggy of Scooby-Doo fame or, when my fuzz is at its absolute best, Yosemite Sam.

I know it took time for Ernest Hemingway, Vincent Van Gogh and Walker Texas Ranger to grow the kind of respectable beard to which I aspire. Yet I also know that Fidel Castro, Jerry Garcia and Colonel Sanders had beards for years and I don't want to look like them.

What I quickly discovered was that for something barely visible, my whiskers itch a lot. It feels like a tiny medieval hair shirt on my face, even though it only looks like I woke up late.

I had almost decided to shave when I began to think about the religious implications. Jesus is always pictured with a beard. "What would Jesus do?" is not a question I wanted to ask.

The biblical witness is predominantly anti-shaving. The most famous trim in scripture, Samson's, was not pro-Barbasol (Judges 16).

The Israelites were told not to shave before a funeral: "You must not lacerate yourselves or shave your forelocks for the dead" (Deut. 14:1).

When Ezra got upset he wrote, "When I heard this, I tore my garment and my mantle, and pulled hair from my head and beard, and sat appalled" (Ezra 9:3). I have never been distressed enough to pull out my own beard, but I imagine it would feel appalling.

The Ammonite King Hanun sent Israelite envoys home after he "shaved off half the beard of each and cut off their garments in the middle at their hips." King David was embarrassed for the men and told them, "Remain at Jericho until your beards have grown" (2 Sam. 10:4-5). Presumably they also found garments that covered their hips.

One prophet wrote that God's heart moans, "For every head is shaved and every beard cut off (Jer. 38:7). Would God moan if I shaved?

Shaving is positive on a few occasions. For instance, "The Nazirites shall shave the consecrated head at the entrance of the tent of meeting, and shall take the hair from the consecrated head and put it on the fire under the sacrifice" (Num. 6:18). Churches that have run out of ways to welcome visitors may want to consider a shave and a haircut followed by a barbecue.

Surely some denomination has split over this — beard-wearers versus clean-shavers. Old German Baptist Brethren do not wear mustaches because they believe it would make them vain, but many grow chest-length beards (which are understandably not a source of pride).

I thought about partial options. I could go with a mustache without a beard (Hitler, Einstein, Ned Flanders from *The Simpsons*), a goatee (Shakespeare, Wolfman Jack, Satan) or a soulpatch (Howie Mandel), but Ned is the only one I look much like. And it was still scratchy.

I know my mother would not like my new fur, but I kept thinking about great beards — Robert E. Lee, Che Guevara, Tim McGraw, Jack Sparrow, Santa, Uncle Sam, Poseidon and Count von Count (from *Sesame Street*).

Some might think I had enough justification for shearing my facial hair, but I kept looking until I found a doctrinal trump card. I was delighted to read the story in which Jacob says to his mother Rebekah, "Look, my brother Esau is a hairy man, but I am a man of smooth skin" (Gen. 27:11). This text clearly teaches that God cares for both the hairy and the smooth. It was time to admit I am no Esau.

I spent two weeks growing my two-day beard. Then I shaved with a clear conscience.

Hair today, gone tomorrow
July 2007

When we moved to Fort Worth and I had to find a new barber, I could picture exactly the kind of barbershop I needed — a red-and-white barber pole, $10 haircuts, 10-year-old copies of *Field and Stream*, a cash register that rings, pocket knives for sale, country music on the radio, the kind of barbershop where only men would be found. My dream barbershop is Floyd's in Mayberry.

The moment I walked in I knew my new barbershop was perfect. The head of a 16-point buck hung on one wall and the Ten Commandments on another. There were five chairs for three barbers — all of whom are older than my dad. Guys with less hair than a peach hung around all day. Gomer could walk in at any minute.

Jerry is an excellent barber. He knows exactly how boring a haircut should be. Our conversations were always the same. He'd ask, "How's the church?" I'd say, "Fine. Just fine. How's your church?"

For years Jerry has been the music director at a church that sounds like every church I grew up in. The only issue with which we had to deal was that, like Floyd, Jerry couldn't cut and talk at the same time. If I asked the wrong question, he might stop cutting for 10 minutes while he answered. I learned to ask yes-and-no questions. I was so happy with my barbershop.

Then a couple of months ago I went for a haircut and the changes had begun. A woman who looked about 25 was seated in one of the empty chairs. It was like seeing Mel Gibson at a synagogue.

I tried to ease into it: "So, Jerry, do you have a new barber?"

Jerry whispered, "She's the new owner."

I smiled, "Well, that's great."

Jerry said, "We'll see."

When I next went to get my hair cut, Jerry was gone. The new owner was the only one there. *Field and Stream* had been replaced by *People*. I didn't recognize the radio station.

I asked, "Can I get a haircut?"

She asked, "Do you see a line?"

"How much will it cost?"

"What was it before?"

"Ten dollars."

"Then that's what it is. How do you want it cut?"

"Six weeks shorter than it is now. My expectations aren't high. I understand you're not working with runway material."

Alexia always wanted to run her own place. She'd hoped the other barbers would stay, but they left to go to other shops. When I asked, "How's business?" she answered, "When people come in and see that it's my shop now, they give me dirty looks and walk out. I don't think old white men want their hair cut by a young Hispanic woman. The only customers I have are the ones who followed me from the old shop in my neighborhood."

Alexia grew up and lives near the stockyards. She does hair coloring as well as ear piercing — which I can't imagine Jerry or Floyd doing. She plans to remove the deer's head, but she hasn't decided on the Ten Commandments. She wants to put in flat screen TVs and set them on ESPN. We talked about boxing, which I no longer know anything about. Apparently George Foreman has retired. When she finished my haircut, she offered to trim my eyebrows — but I'm just not ready for that.

In six weeks I'll go back to Alexia for a haircut, because I have enough people to talk about church with and I don't know many from her part of town. I understand the people who drive across town to stick with their old barbers. Sometimes we want what we've gotten used to. The only problem with staying with those who make us feel at ease is that every once in a while God pushes us to something different, even if it's just a trim.